Madonna King is one of Australia's most accomplished journalists, having worked at senior levels at News Limited and the ABC, where she presented the *Mornings* program in Brisbane for six years. Madonna writes for Fairfax and has a regular radio spot on Brisbane's 4BC. She has written eight books, all defined by her skilful reporting and her ability to get people to talk in depth. Her 2017 bestseller, *Being 14*, was shortlisted for the ABIA Award for General Non-Fiction Book of the Year. Madonna is also a parent of two teenage girls.

madonnaking.com.au
@madonnamking

ALSO BY MADONNA KING

Think Smart Run Hard: Lessons in Business Leadership from Maxine Horne

Hockey: Not Your Average Joe

Ian Frazer: The Man Who Saved a Million Lives

A Generous Helping: Treasured Recipes from the People of Queensland (with Alison Alexander)

Bali 9: The Untold Story (with Cindy Wockner)

Catalyst: The Power of the Media and the Public to Make Change

Being 14: Helping Fierce Teens Become Awesome Women

MADONNA KING

FATHERS
AND
DAUGHTERS

Helping girls and their dads
build unbreakable bonds

hachette
AUSTRALIA

Published in Australia and New Zealand in 2018
by Hachette Australia
(an imprint of Hachette Australia Pty Limited)
Level 17, 207 Kent Street, Sydney NSW 2000
www.hachette.com.au

10 9 8 7 6 5 4 3 2 1

A catalogue record for this
book is available from the
National Library of Australia

NATIONAL
LIBRARY
OF AUSTRALIA

ISBN: 978 0 7336 4020 9 (paperback)

Cover design by Christabella Designs
Cover photograph courtesy of Getty Images
Typeset in 12.2/18.6 pt Sabon LT Std by Bookhouse, Sydney
Printed and bound in Australia by McPherson's Printing Group

*To dads, granddads, uncles and everyone else who
believes in the magic of our girls.*

Contents

1

Fathers and daughters

Rebecca is nominating her earliest memory of her father. 'Dad made me a doll's house,' she says. 'He wanted me to have a big wooden one and all my friends had little plastic ones. He wanted mine to be the best.' Stacey chimes in, relating early memories of her dad patiently teaching her to ride a boogie board. Alison tells of how she was thrown high in the air while mucking around in the family's pool. Emily used to hide under the covers and her father would pretend that he couldn't find her. And Hannah? 'I remember when we were little we would go to Grandpa's place and Dad would be watching the cricket on his back,' she says. She tells of how she would happily climb all over him. 'I was about five.' Now, a decade or so later, these girls, like so many of their peers, are travelling through the tunnel of teen-dom. Anxiety is crippling some of them, and body image issues afflicting others. The smiles of some are being stolen by friends, who turn into tormentors without warning. And bullying is sabotaging the adolescence of many. Their phone is their friend some days and their adversary on others. It's a world they know is remarkably different from that of their parents; one that they know their dad, in particular, couldn't possibly understand.

For these girls, who grew up in families with predominantly traditional gender roles, their fathers were their all at age five: the superhero who swept in each afternoon and tucked them in at night; the booming voice of authority that could fix anything. They knew, even then, that in his eyes they could do no wrong. Now, that was tipped on its head. Dad had become distant; a bit like a stranger. He provided for the family, funded a good part of the mortgage and turned up at the netball final. But he worked longer hours now than she could ever remember. She wouldn't dare plop herself down beside him and talk about the wild hormones that took hold of her happiness on some days, or the first stirrings of interest in the boy at the bus shelter. She doesn't even know how that conversation could begin! Weeks would pass, sometimes, without her and her father sitting down together and talking, uninterrupted, for ten minutes. She knew he loved her, but she resented him being overprotective and the fact that he was a Luddite when it came to understanding Instagram. Even his jokes, which once sent her into fits of giggles, were no longer funny. Actually, they were *really* embarrassing.

Fathers, too, feel that cold change. This is his daughter; the girl who tailed him around the backyard all morning each Saturday. He was her soldier, her superhero, her defender. She was his offsider, who would walk up to the school gate clutching his hand. She would confide in him, race to greet him at the end of the day and laugh at every 'dad joke' he told. She'd spend hours perfecting that dance she would put on for the family, and even longer planning the messy breakfast she'd serve up each Father's Day. Then, without notice, and somewhere between her tenth and fourteenth birthday, she'd changed. Or something had happened. It didn't happen in one day but over a period of time in a way that disguised its impact. He remembers her uneasily removing her hand from his on a Monday in June a few years ago. The new and staggering influence of her friends bewildered him. Social media, too: Facebook, Snapchat, Instagram and a host of others whose names he couldn't recall but whose influence was pervasive. Together, her friends and her phone seemed to dictate what clothes she should wear and what music she should download. The number of 'likes' on her Instagram account became a touchstone to her moods. One moment life was perfect, the next pathetic. Those long, lovely talks they'd shared stopped, too. Yes, his work had intervened, for sure, but the mortgage had fallen as a result. Maybe he'd stepped back a bit, particularly at the very start of adolescence when she stopped being so forthcoming. Her mother had a lived experience at being a girl. He didn't. He'd sit on the sidelines for a bit and hope she returned to him once this teenage trip had passed . . .

Fathers and daughters: despite everything, it is a relationship built on a certain strain of magic. That doesn't mean other parent–child relationships aren't as valuable or don't bring as much joy. Of course they do, and each of them offers their own unique charm. But the father–daughter bond can be as captivating as it is challenging – and almost impossible to measure. 'There's something special about a father–daughter relationship, and when you look at the research no-one can really explain it,' says Paul Dillon, founder of Drug and Alcohol Research and Training Australia. Yet research is able to quantify its power. Fathers can raise their daughters' academic performance. They can influence, hugely, who they choose as a future partner. A good father–daughter relationship can do so much more than that, too. It can empower daughters to believe in themselves and to prosecute a case with conviction and confidence. It can bestow upon a girl a sense of belonging, a self-efficacy and a resilience for life. It can teach her mindfulness and reason, along with how to change a light bulb and a car tyre. That doesn't mean that mothers can't provide those lessons. Nor does it mean that those same lessons can't be taught by other males in a girl's life. They can be.

Research has proved fathers struggle more than mothers with emotional cues. Children see the differences in their parents, too. While at the age of eight they might talk to both about the same things, girls say they are more likely to seek Mum out as an adolescent. They will go to Dad, they say, when they want to canvass options in a clinical way. Mum will invest more emotion in their lives; affairs of the heart will be principally her domain. Dad figures he doesn't need to know the names of her friends, and is unlikely to lose sleep over a friendship issue. He doesn't see the need, either, to follow her on social media, even if he knew how to. Those differences, between mothers and fathers, will almost always spill over into parenting, and a couple will see different challenges, hold mismatched expectations and want to approach issues in varied ways. That can test any parenting partnership, but it can also strain father–daughter unions.

A generational divide means that daughters and their fathers live in divergent worlds too. His, more than likely, has been unchanged for years. He has a daily and weekly routine, and views formed over years. Hers might be the polar opposite, filled with changing friendships, a wi-fi world of devices and apps, instant gratification, and fashion fads.

So how does a father navigate parenting his daughter, while keeping that magic alive? And what can daughters do to make it work? They are the questions I've set out to answer with this book, after surveying about 1200 girls, aged ten to seventeen, and almost 400 fathers, aged between thirty-eight and sixty-six, who had daughters. More than one hundred additional teen girls were then interviewed, to discuss the answers given by their peers, as well as 60 mothers. The advice of dozens and dozens of teen experts – school principals, wellbeing officers and counsellors, teen psychologists, education consultants, parenting experts and police – was also sought.

Generalisations are impossible to escape here. Many girls pass through adolescence without a blip and the relationship they share with their fathers is unbreakable. Increasingly, families are also made up of two mothers or two fathers, and step-families can be as common as nuclear families. With 617,000 one-parent families with dependent children being recorded in the 2016 Census, the role of step-fathers is elephantine. So, in focusing on fathers and their daughters, it's important not to undervalue any other family make-ups. But the idea for this book was decided when a father challenged me after a parenting talk in Adelaide. Having chatted about my previous book *Being 14*, I was racing to catch a plane. This father, who has a daughter and a step-daughter, pursued me to the car. 'I've tried everything,' he said. 'Really everything. Just tell me what else I can do to re-connect with my girls!'

No doubt exists in my mind that many fathers are lost, and want to retrieve a relationship that was once wrapped in gold. When asked what they wanted advice on, their answers covered the spectrum: how to encourage their daughter to look at long-term goals, not this weekend's splurge; how to love herself (which one father described as a 'unicorn hunt'); how to coax her out of her room; how to talk to her about body image and tormentors masquerading as friends, and how to understand her anxiety. Take these examples:

'I wish I could find a way to talk to her about her weight without the risk of it looking like some sort of self-image, fat-shaming exercise. It isn't that at all, just a concern for her health.'

'I really know nothing about her life as she is a closed book and secretive. She is unwilling to let me be involved as she is now almost independent and no longer reliant on me to help her get around to where she wants to go.'

'I am finding the whole girlfriend-set clique to be confusing. Both of my daughters can come home from school in tears because of a friend-set issue. It seems to me that these types of occurrences have a greater effect

*on girls, whereas boys might not take it the same way,
or maybe they are just not expressing it.'*

But the biggest issue on which fathers sought advice was social media. One explained his concern about a 'new paradigm where people publish an edited version of their life for the world to see. I am starting to see signs,' he continued, 'in slightly older people, of an increasing discontentment and competitiveness as they want the perfect edited lives their friends portray. I suspect this will evolve to be a very negative and destructive side of an otherwise useful tool.' Others worry about the influence of Instagram and Snapchat, and the risk-taking behaviour they believe it prompts. 'She has been abused online by teenage boys and I was planning to show the messages to the police, however she insisted that she didn't want me to do that, even though she was being threatened,' one father says.

When fathers were asked to nominate the number-one concern they had for their daughter/s, a unanimity of views popped up. Peer group pressure. Poor judgement. Her safety. An inexplicable anxiety. Social media. Bullying. Boys. Sex. Drugs. Her self-image. An addiction to YouTube and 'likes' on Instagram, while eschewing the classics. Finding acceptance among her friends.

Tony says he just wants his daughter to be at peace with her appearance. 'Like most girls her age, she is always wishing her skin, her eyes, her hair were in some way different and more beautiful,' he says. It's friendships that has Dave confused: 'I sometimes am concerned that she feels the need to be with who she perceives as "the cool girls" when, in my opinion, they may not be the best people for her.' Grant says this: 'I have noticed a real difference between boys and girls, with girls being much more callous than boys.'

Ask girls about the role they want their fathers to play in their lives and the congruence of their answers is likewise striking. They want their father to be home more. To be present. 'He's always at work,' Trudy says. 'He's never really around much,' says Evie. They want their fathers to at least try and talk to them more, even if they are rebuffed. They want to do stuff, like go for a run, or a hike, or go out to dinner. They want their father to understand that they might have different views, and that they want to be trusted more than over-protected. They want to be parented like their brothers. They want their fathers to know that they admire how rational they are, and that their responses rarely overdramatise an issue. But they wish their dads would turn up more to school functions, and work less. At fourteen and fifteen and sixteen, she won't say it, but she misses the magic of being eight, when her father was still her hero. 'He is the awesomest daddy in the world. He loves me very much.' Meg, aged ten, says. 'A big fluffy bear hugger,' says Shelly.

'Things may be going bad, but then SWOOSH, my dad is there to help. He's like a secret superhero. His name would be Captain Crazy Dad.' Or this: 'My dad is like shelter on a stormy night. His hugs are the best.' These girls are all prepubescent and yet to wage that daily war with their hormones. By their early to mid teens, their relationship with their dad will change. Some girls say it becomes 'cordial'. Others believe it goes to custard.

They stop talking to their fathers in the way they once did. And finding personal conversations and their daughter's change in personality difficult to navigate, fathers often take a big step back, too. 'Once upon a time, pre-puberty, we were best mates,' one dad says. 'I believe by the time she finishes her tertiary education we will be again. That's life.' At this point, in many homes, Dad becomes more the provider than the parent. More the comic than the genial confidant. The disciplinarian, not the decider. But after listening to so many fathers and daughters, it's clear that how a father handles this tricky period will play a large part in determining the relation-ship once she has matured. The gap will close quickly, if he stays close despite daily brush-offs. But girls whose fathers left the room when they turned twelve find it difficult to open the door as wide, at fifteen or sixteen or even nineteen. That evidence provided in the course of my research was anecdotal – but overwhelming.

Separations and divorce can make this father–daughter trip even more ticklish. 'He's great. In fact, I love him to the moon and back without the influence of his girlfriend. But with her, I don't even want to know him,' Alison says, for example. With a wisdom beyond their years, many girls also point to their father's own background as an indicator of why he parents the way he does. 'My father always says to us kids, "I am hard/strict on you kids because I want you all to have what I didn't when I was younger and I want the best for you all,"' Molly says. Freya sees it this way: 'He came from a family that wasn't wealthy and lived on a farm. That's taught him to be really resourceful. He says everything that is broken can be fixed.' And fathers who experienced painful or difficult or unsupported childhoods set out to fix that, for their own children.

Roles are changing, too, and this doesn't make it trouble-free for any parent. While mothers still bear the brunt of housework and child rearing, fathers are increasingly realising that providing is not parenting. Some are quitting their jobs, or declining promotions, or working around school functions. They're a minority still, but some are butting up against a glass ceiling in their daughter's lives in the same way their partners might be trying to smash it in their workplaces. Employers still see male workers, not fathers; and mothers, too, can find it difficult to share the huge investment they've made in the home, often at the expense of work promotions. Both are challenged by a parenting world that requires talents and skills their own parents didn't need.

Catherine O'Kane, the principal of All Hallows' School in Brisbane, talks about agility in parenting, in the same way agile leadership is the corporate term *du jour*. Increasingly, digital firecrackers at work are demanding greater adaptability and innovation. So why wouldn't those same skills be needed at home, to parent a two-year-old boy, and a sixteen-year-old girl? The skill sets involved there are strikingly different, and the smartphone and what it can deliver adds to that complexity. But how many fathers tuck into a parenting book for advice? Indeed, it's more likely that a teacher of teenagers will have parenting books plastered across his or her desk than a father (or perhaps even a mother) will. That's a recognition of the important role schools now play in teen girls' lives, but also of the particular challenges faced by teachers tasked with educating adolescents.

Educators show a strong insight into the problems faced by their students' fathers. Dr Linda Evans, Toowoomba's Fairholme College principal, says fathers can be wrong-footed by their girls, who might go from being the apple of their eye to 'feisty and manipulative and unpredictable and volatile and sensitive and very difficult to read'. 'They have to understand what's going on,' Dr Evans says. 'If they're not dealing with it, they actually have to do something to address that.' Tom Matthews, who is the head of guidance counselling at St Andrew's College in Christchurch, says he learns something from his teen daughter daily. 'I think as a father if we're not changing and learning as much as our daughters, we're doing it wrong. If we want our daughters to be better than us and be with partners better than us and to be better parents than us, then we have to not be just equal but better than them with self-reflection and learning, and model stuff like apologising.'

Kevin Tutt, the head of Seymour College in Adelaide, says schools have recognised the need for fathers to engage with their daughters and have become 'an agency for it'. A principal for twenty-six years, he sees fathers as being able to impact upon their daughters' academic, sporting and cultural achievements, as well as their mental health, particularly in the areas of resilience, self-reliance and assertiveness. 'I base that on anecdotal evidence that girls with a strong relationship with their dads tend to be more confident, more resilient, more mentally well. Their sense of wellbeing is strong,' he says.

But how do men find their place? Often, their partners have become the family CEO, organising home affairs and leading the parenting. Rigorous protection policies can also limit fathers having the same involvement that mothers might enjoy at school. It's an awkward place for a father, wanting to engage with his daughter. 'Dads are looking for help,' says Linda Douglas, principal of Ruyton Girls' School in Melbourne. 'It's a matter of working out how they will feel supported and not battered down. Over the last however-many years, it has been a difficult terrain for men to work out where their place is.' Men might line up at the rowing, but fewer show up regularly at netball. 'These places have been traditionally owned by women simply because of the way our society has functioned, and so the men have now got to come into the places and work out the social nuances ... it's not straightforward,' she says.

Social researcher Mark McCrindle says fathers whose whole experience is Australian-based are being required to parent a 'global generation' of teenagers. 'It's just not about knowing the local bands like INXS or Midnight Oil, or whoever it might have been for the dads of today, but keeping across what is a very fast-changing global context,' he says. 'That's true of brands, of how they shop, of news and entertainment. It has created more gaps and a contextual challenge for dads to find that common ground.' Fathers and daughters use different language and consume content in entirely different ways. 'We call them Generation Glass because it's the glass that they touch and tap on,' he says. Most fathers would have envisaged a parenthood where their daughters read magazines, watched videos and were engaged in a school system with textbooks. 'The emergence of the screen-ager and touch screens has probably taken the dads by surprise,' he says. Even homework, where a dad might have added value, now required expertise in Moodle, class blogs and a school app. Mr Google has replaced some dads as the go-to person. 'All of that has wrong-footed dads and created a connection challenge,' McCrindle says. 'I think dads, particularly those with teenage daughters, are trying to find their place and trying to shape some values that have been foundational for them in a world that is moving very quickly.'

Dr Justin Coulson, author of *10 Things Every Parent Needs to Know*, says today's fathers remain oblivious to the enormous influence they nevertheless have on their daughters. 'Too many dads feel as though they are a walking wallet and as a result of that they don't recognise how vital their daily involvement with their daughters is,' he says. 'They don't recognise that if they can be a light in their daughters' lives, their daughters are much more likely to feel good about themselves, they're much more likely to do well at school, they're far less likely to have an eating disorder, they're far less likely to suffer from anxiety, and they're far more likely to communicate because of the trust and the bond that's been built.'

Sounds like a big gig, so where does a father in the 21st century start?

2

Changing times

Dr Steve Hambleton, a Brisbane GP, remembers his young patient vividly. She had sat across from his desk and opened her heart. She hated herself, she told him. She hated everything she was doing. Dr Hambleton pauses. 'Nobody knew,' he says. 'Not a soul knew.' Not her parents. Not her teachers. This former head of the Australian Medical Association asked his patient why she hadn't confided in someone earlier. 'I didn't tell anyone because I hated myself,' she said. Dr Hambleton, who has three daughters and a son of his own, tells the story to illustrate the point that parents need to understand the pressures teen girls feel. In his three decades of practising medicine, of being involved in government policy and of raising daughters of his own, there's one thing he sees as the biggest current concern for girls aged ten to seventeen:

self-esteem. 'That's number one,' says Dr Hambleton. 'And you won't know unless you look for it.'

The journey a girl takes from the ages of ten to seventeen is unlike any other one, and it can turn their life – and those who love them – upside down. They might love their parents at sunrise and be mortified by them at sundown. A poorly timed or random comment from a classmate can mean they'll dissolve into tears. The highs can be Herculean but the lows are just as deep. One moment they'll be a chatterbox, like they were in primary school, the next moment they're mute, in their room with the door slammed shut. Theirs is a world where bullying and social exclusion can be common, where the power of celebrity beats all, and where twenty-four-hour connectivity can boost their education, access and security, but also rule their lives by dominating their sleep patterns and academic results, determining their friendships and shaping how they see themselves as young women. Many girls will compare themselves to the images that dominate the wallpaper of marketing that pops up on their smartphone, and they'll regularly judge their worth by how many followers they have on social media. They will want everything with yesterday's speed, instant gratification being the diet fed to them since birth. Much of their behaviour will be self-centred. For fathers, even more of it will be indecipherable. 'Adolescents live rainbows,' Dr Hambleton says. 'Everything is by colours. Sadness is really sad. Happiness is really happy. If you want to write a song, get an adolescent to write the lyrics! But maintaining self-esteem is hard – especially as the inter-action with parents changes. So many parents will say to me, "But they don't talk to me anymore", "I don't know what they're thinking".'

That change is as difficult for fathers as it is for their daughters. At ten, many girls will still hold Dad's hand at the school gate. But that will stop, along with his authority, in many cases. And he will become 'so embarrassing'. 'My father was wearing thongs at a school barbecue. Do you believe it?' Aimie, twelve, says. 'My dad wears a beanie and a hat at the same time so that he's warm and sun-safe!' says Ally, fourteen. Dr Linda Evans explains the ten- to seventeen-year-old journey in this way: 'A ten-year-old still wants to play. A ten-year-old isn't conscious of how she looks to someone else. For a ten-year-old it's about play and friendship with girls. Boys haven't come into the equation.' Girls of this age are innocent of life's com-plexities and are still strongly attached to their parents. 'At seventeen, they're desperately seeking independence and they want to find their independent self,' continues Dr Evans. 'They want to define themselves differently from their mother, first and foremost, and they seek the approval of their peer group over their parents.'

Diana Vernon, principal of Methodist Ladies' College in Melbourne, is a biologist and she sees girls as turning from keen and wide-eyed caterpillars, where the world and everything in it is marvellous, into butterflies, ready to own the world. 'Around Years 8 and 9 they go into what I call the chrysalis stage,' she says. That's where tantrums and eye-rolling might become part of their daily repertoire. 'They don't want to be little girls because that's not cool, and being grown up is really boring. They're trying to find their identity,' she says. Life, at school and home, can become awkward. 'They still want that little girl hug, but not in front of anybody else,' Vernon says. 'They desperately need that support, even if they present as being prickly.' That chrysalis stage can be indecipherable and indeterminate but they do at last fly out of school as butterflies, engaging with adults and seeing their parents as individuals, as well as Mum and Dad.

What you see is not always what you get, either. On the outside, a teen girl might present as determined and strong and wilful. But underneath that bravado, many of our girls are feeling lost, anxious, unsure. A girl might battle to find friends and even when she does she'll still have times when she feels utterly alone. Home is no longer a sanctuary for her; social media follows her everywhere – testing her, exciting her, connecting her and sometimes being a weapon used against her. At the same time, she'll feel captive to the changes wreaking havoc with her body. The physical changes are obvious, but they come with a raft of emotional, social and cognitive changes. The list of questions she's asking herself runs to pages, and she struggles with many of the answers. Will she get her period for the first time on school camp? Who will she tell if it happens at school? Will she find a partner for the school dance? What will she wear? How do girls get a boyfriend? How many 'likes' did she get on her last post? Why does this teacher hate her? Why does she feel sad and anxious sometimes, when everyone around her is having fun? Why? Why? Why?

Mothers will understand much of this, minus the pervasive influence of social media. They will understand the highs and the lows, and the changes that steal certainty out of each day. But fathers, with no lived experience of the physiological changes, can feel lost and challenged. Linda Douglas says fathers begin that journey into adolescence with their daughter wanting to sit on his lap or asking to hold his hand. 'The next minute it's like, "Don't come near me." Negotiating the world of an adolescent girl . . . we should all be doing a degree on that!'

The average age of puberty has grown younger over time, and now sits at twelve. In many cases, girls begin menstruating at age eleven. It's about this time that all the secondary sexual characteristics begin to change. She will begin to develop breasts and pubic hair. Her hips might begin to widen and her arms and legs to lengthen. Dr Katherine Main, senior lecturer in the School of Education and Professional Studies at Queensland's

Griffith University, observes that it can be a difficult time for girls. 'They might have been somebody who was very good at tennis, for example, and then they go through a significant growth spurt in about eighteen months where they can put on 10 per cent or more of their weight, put on 10 cm in height and all of a sudden everything is out of whack. Their centre of gravity is different, the length of their arms is different, and so they struggle with who they are and this new clumsiness.' Do girls understand these changes? 'Often there's a mismatch between the physiological age and the psychological age, and you can have an eleven-year-old who is looking like an adult woman but she's got the brain of an eleven-year-old,' Dr Hambleton says. 'That's really quite awkward, because people overestimate their ability to cope.' Dr Main agrees, saying that girls develop – physically, emotionally, socially and cognitively – more between the ages of twelve and sixteen than at any other time, bar the first few years of life. It's not only the development of breasts, hips, body hair and body odour. For many, an attraction to boys begins, and some girls grapple with a warped sense of their own body image.

At the beginning, periods can be all over the place, presenting logistical problems but also causing an enormous sense of unease. Girls say this is a difficult issue to broach, even with their peers. Dr Hambleton says he notes the relief on girls' faces when he tells them that 'abnormal is absolutely normal' at the start. It can take two years to develop a regular menstrual cycle, or even longer. The variable levels of sharing about the topic in friendship groups can make matters worse: wrong information is swapped and some girls believe something is wrong with them.

The onset of menstruation can be associated with mood swings. 'You get a big surge of female hormones that fluctuate over a cycle and that leave you in a hormone-withdrawal state for some of the time, and an overdose at other times,' Dr Hambleton says. Just as girls are trying to find where they belong, their body is acting up. Emotionally they are starting to change because of those hormonal changes – they might be more sensitive, each day becomes a roller-coaster ride of feelings, and they have a greater allegiance to their peers. School workloads are increasing, and relationships can become more complex. At the same time they are trying to function as part of a peer group where others are riding the same wild changes. That friend who is the source of great support on some days can be the source of great pain on others. Middle school teachers, those in the years between primary and senior school, know this well. An altercation between a group of girls at lunchtime can mean afternoon lessons are futile, and those on lunchtime duty look out for telltale signs: girls who are feeling ostracised, or not fitting in, or are the subject of others' taunts. 'It stands out, pretty much,' one teacher says. 'But that doesn't make it easy to deal with.' A lack of sleep – caused by night-time social media excursions or a heavy extracurricular program – in many instances adds to those mood swings. 'One day it might be one girl, the next day it's another in her group having a hard time. It's like they are in a heightened sensory orbit the whole time,' a school counsellor says.

In adolescence, risk-taking behaviours can increase. This is particularly the case between the ages of twelve and twenty-five. At this time, the connections from one part of the brain to another become more efficient from the bottom to the top and from the front to the back – in that order. The frontal cortex helps a person organise and plan, ensuring we consider the consequences of our actions, governing our judgement and our reasoning powers, self-regulation, logic and impulse. It is during these crucial years that this part of the brain is still developing. For that reason, we might see a teen finding it difficult to organise their school homework, or making a silly and impulsive decision, or acting like an eight-year-old one day and a twenty-three-year-old the next. Often, as adults, we can be quick to jump to judgement on that – but we would do well to listen to the scientists, who are more forgiving of our teens because of their understanding of how the brain grows and develops. During the teen years and as the brain develops, emotional responses can leap out of the stalls first, and the push for independence becomes strong. Egocentric, their moral compasses are maturing too, and at different paces. Dr Katherine Main says this can be a delightful time. 'During that thirteen- to fourteen-year period they turn from doing what's right because they're worried about getting into trouble if they do what's wrong, to doing what's right because it's the right thing to do. That's where we see them getting involved in causes – environmental sustainability and save the whales,' she says. She says adolescence is changing and extending, at both ends. It is starting earlier, because of factors like better nutrition, but it is extending, socially, at the other end. Our children are students longer, and enter 'adulthood' later, and that means the roles and responsibilities change at different ages – and adults need to understand that. 'We want them to be grown up but we don't give them the opportunity to take risks and understand the consequences of that,' Dr Main says. 'We are robbing them of opportunities to learn resilience.'

The technology changing the world also adds a complexity, from an early age. 'What they have shown is that as they are using more and more technology, their brains are wiring differently from older generations, and there's also an inverse response in terms of their social and emotional development.' Because they are doing more online, and they are using less face-to-face contact, their social skills aren't developing as well.

Another important change that occurs at the age of ten or so concerns a child's understanding of 'permanence'. Before the age of eight or nine or ten, children are not able to think in the abstract. They might not understand long-term planning, or the concept of permanence. Life is black and white, simple and straightforward. But that changes at around ten, particularly if a child loses a grandparent. Until that point the child might not even have understood that death is permanent. The common reaction of a seven- or eight-year-old to seeing a parent upset is to believe that they've done something wrong; that it is their fault, Dr Hambleton says. 'They might have yelled at Grandma or thought ill of Grandma and therefore believed it was their fault that she had died.' He says this is difficult for parents, already grieving an elderly parent. But at ten or eleven, children begin to realise that death is forever, and that can bring on another line of anxiety. 'They might then think, "OMG, my mum is going to die one day; what will I do?"' he says.

All of this is harder because girls stop talking as openly as they did earlier on. 'It happens so suddenly, you don't realise it,' one father says. 'You are driving to work and the banter changes. It's different.' 'Forget the birds and the bees talk,' says another father, '*they're* more likely to be able to tell *you*!' Dr Hambleton has his own story. He was driving his daughters to school each morning, reciting desk calendar sayings. 'When it rains, look for rainbows. When it's dark, look for stars,' he might say. Or, 'Mistakes are proof that you are trying.' His daughters would hang off every word. Then one morning he remembers announcing that 'if you follow crowds, crowds will never follow you'. The aphorism was met by silence, and then, 'What are you talking about, Dad?' His dad jokes received similar feedback around the same time.

It's at this point that many fathers decide to hand the complexity over to their partners, with relief. That's not a good idea, according to every bit of research and every expert interviewed for this project. Stepping back or opting out can make it mighty difficult in a few years' time when he wants to 'step back in'. This concept has been stated already, and is repeated in chapters that follow; but it's a critical point. When the physical, psychological, emotional and cognitive changes kick in and girls begin to pull away from their fathers, whose authority they no longer see as insurmountable, this is not the time for fathers to sit on the sidelines. These answers – to the question of whether they had noticed a change in the relationship with their father over the previous two years – are all from girls aged twelve to fourteen.

'It has changed a little as I am entering my teen years.'

'Yes. The stresses of being a teenager and the stereotypes associated with that have changed our relationship.'

'Yes, we have drifted apart.'

'Yes, it has deteriorated.'

'Yes, I don't tell him as much.'

'Yes, it's more distant.'

'I feel less comfortable talking to him about things that I might have previously been able to.'

'Yes, I have become less "close" with my dad. We fight a lot more and I have started to get angry with him lately.'

'As I am becoming a young woman, I have become a bit more independent and do not share some things with him anymore.'

'I'm an only child so I used to treat Dad almost like a brother. We'd "playful fight" a lot. But now that I've matured we don't have as much to talk about.'

These girls, embarking on adolescence, feel as though they've lost the father they've known for the first decade. And he, no doubt, feels it too. A few years later they start to see things a little differently. All of the statements following come from girls aged fifteen to seventeen.

'I'm closer than I was last year. I hope it continues because it's kind of nice not fighting all the time.'

'I hug my dad in public now. I didn't do that in middle school!'

'I have learnt to listen to him more. He is actually right about more than I thought.'

'I never used to get along with him a lot, but now we are great friends.'

Catching up on those lost years is all the more difficult if the connection deteriorated too much during puberty. Re-finding a place at a daughter's side might not be as easy as it sounds.

'To be perfectly honest, I miss the relationship I once had with my father.'

'Over the past two years I felt a drift away from my father and am trying to come back. This most likely occurred due to a clash in ideas, as I try to make my own decisions and form choices in what I think is right and wrong, possibly disagreeing with what he believes.'

'Yes, we were once very close and he was openly affectionate, but now that I am older we have grown more distant. I think he is put off by me growing up and not being his little girl anymore.'

'Sorry, there's no going back.'

More often than not, in cases where fathers and daughters were strongly connected at seventeen, their fathers didn't take a break from parenting along the way. He put his little girl to bed at six, treated her like a young woman at thirteen, grew her confidence when she needed it at fourteen, understood the first stirrings of interest in boys at fifteen, and continually wanted to undertake activities with her.

> *'He helps me with homework and is sometimes my favourite teacher. This is a major difference, as previously we would have played games instead of doing work together!'*

> *'I feel like I can share more with him because he knows I'm changing and growing up, and he's understanding and helpful about it.'*

However, the difficulty for fathers – and mothers – is knowing when something is 'normal' and when it might require more serious attention. Or what is a show, and what's not. 'It's very hard to pick,' Dr Hambleton admits. 'You have to be really sensitive. You've got to listen; you've got to look for clues.' And sometimes the best way to do that, according to parenting experts and school counsellors, is to develop an informal parents' network with your daughter's friends' parents. In primary school, that was easy. Parents saw each other in school drop-off lines and at birthday parties. We'd check with each other on issues ranging from school lunch boxes to what they needed to wear on a class excursion. But once children head off to high school, that contact lessens: the school might not be local, or they travel by public transport; their friends might live on the other side of town. Dropping that adult contact can come at a real cost. 'Would you like to know if your kid was blind drunk on a school night at the age of twelve?' Dr Hambleton asks me this question. My answer is an emphatic 'Yes, of course!' He continues: 'Our kids are going to grow up, they're going to cross all the bridges we crossed, and parents should ask themselves that question – would they like to know? Because plenty of times everyone knows except for Mum or Dad.' Mothers are often more in that loop than fathers and are more likely to run a view by another parent. But are our parent networks strong enough that we would discover if our daughter was having sex with someone at the age of fourteen? Or that she was sneaking out to meet friends when we believed she was in bed? 'Would I like to know?' Dr Hambleton is asking himself the same question: as a GP, a parent, and a father. 'Yes, I would!' So why don't we pick up the phone to each other? Why don't fathers meet and chat about their daughters in the same way mothers sometimes do? Why do we think a child embarking on seriously risky behaviour is not the business of all of us?

For a father to stay close to his daughter through puberty requires hard work. He needs to understand the changes she is experiencing. He needs to accept there will be times when her mood is unreadable. He needs to accept *her*. This is not an easy task. Over the previous few years, his daughter has faced vast changes – physical, emotional and hormonal. Her brain has changed. Her friends have likely changed (sometimes several times). The amount of change might not have played such a big role in his childhood. It was more marked by time and space and events. We might have been in high school in the 1980s, played cricket in big backyards, with a hills hoist hosting the family's washing. We remember events – like the fall of the Berlin Wall, or the vote against the republic, or the 2000 Olympic Games, or the end of innocence on September 11, 2001. Technology has quashed what a generation means for our daughters. Trends rise and fall with a celebrity's status. So does language. Communication is now via text, or photo. And then a daughter enters adolescence, introducing a variable that can turn the house on its head. How her father handles that as she turns ten or eleven or twelve will be a key factor in how she comes out the other end at fifteen or sixteen or seventeen.

That relationship has to be built on both understanding and agility, as she goes from singing into a plastic microphone to rolling her eyes at his jokes. He needs to understand that she might be in the eye of a cyclone, brought on by a changing body, a growing brain, a new attraction to someone, a flare-up in old friend-ships, a bigger school workload, a search for her own identity and a loss of that self-confidence that shone a few years earlier. She will also be seeking greater independence; a contradiction, given that these girls will want to make their own decisions while still being totally financially tied to their parents. She might lash out. 'It's not what they want to say at all but they'll say it because that's their emotional response, and then they back themselves into a corner,' Dr Main says. 'You have to be able to give them a way out. That fight-or-flight response is probably their first response to any challenge.'

Experts urge fathers to be open, based on the rationale that if they are, their girls will be more likely to feel they can be open also. The advice to accept them for who they are will not always be easy. 'Sometimes we don't give them enough credit for who they are at that point in time,' Dr Main says. 'What we do is we ask them what they want to be when they grow up – yet they're great now! At fourteen they're doing amazing things. They show great leadership and take on responsibilities in a whole range of different areas, and yet we don't tend to be accepting.' Another expert says that sometimes, if fathers aren't accepting, their daughter will seek approval elsewhere. She warns that that could be in the arms of a young male peer. Or, conversely, they might try to excel in an area that was important to her father, not something she enjoys doing herself. With a passion for art, she might try hockey – just to get her father's attention. 'So much depends on how dads deal with them during that time,' Dr Main says. 'They can either see him as someone who's been supportive of them or they can see him as someone who's been totally disengaged and disconnected to them and their reality.'

Principal Linda Douglas says that by the age of seventeen, re-engagement can be strong. She sees it as her students graduate. 'You watch our girls when they finish Year 12 – and it's a pretty emotional time – and in many ways it's no different to when they were in Year 6 at a celebration. They do come out of that tunnel,' she says. 'It's a wonderful thing.'

Understanding. Not painting her into a corner. Listening. Looking hard for cues that show a significant difference in behaviour. Being engaged with her friends' parents and her school. Accepting her. Those skills are the best ones available to beat the inevitable challenges that will surface. Dr Hambleton returns to the story of his young female patient who fought her way out of a difficult adolescence. 'This particular girl decided she was going to end her life.

She shut down her Facebook, said goodbye to everyone. Thankfully one of her friends alerted her family and it was averted. But she had no self-esteem. She thought she was worthless. She thought she was ugly.' She just didn't know how to tell anyone.

3

How dads see their daughters

Neil remembers his toddler daughters running around the house in fairy dresses and playing princesses. Cubbies made from sheets draped over furniture played a key role in their make-believe games. 'As a father, you enjoy it, but it's a bit alien to you,' he says.

Before they walk through the school gates for the first time, fathers are the giants of young girls' worlds. Big and brave and bold – children nearly always describe their father in glowing terms. Physically, he is like a mountain to them, and fathers feel that too. They see themselves as their daughters' 'protector', their size meaning they are able to remove their children from danger with a swoop of their arms. Jason remembers the enormous changes prompted by the birth of both of his daughters, now aged eight and ten. 'When we left the hospital and had to put the baby in the car and drive home, we were paranoid someone was going to crash into us,' he says. 'Then we got home, and our whole life changed.' Long nights chatting to his wife, or watching television, were assigned to history. '[The baby] became the complete centre of attention – but it's going by in a flash. I can't believe how fast they are growing up.' Andrew, the father of four girls aged fourteen, eleven, nine and five, says their current ages chart that trajectory. The youngest one still puts on dances and shows for him and his wife to attend, when once they were all involved. 'The older ones now don't do that; they're more into their friends,' he says, 'facetiming and spending time in their room.'

In the blink of an eye, fathers see their young girls turn to technology, many of them becoming screen junkies staring at screens for at least three hours a day by the age of twelve to thirteen. Technology can be superb for their education, but fathers see their personal influence, and the time their daughter wants to spend with them, begin to wane. The girls become more interested in clothes in a way that fathers find hard to fathom: they know brands, and clothing shops, and can be particular about their tastes. The princess costume is filed at the bottom of the cupboard. 'You turn around one day and the little girl who was running around in a fairy costume is looking quite sassy for an eight-year-old,' Neil says, 'and you think, "She's bloody grown up on me!"' Neil has three daughters, twenty-five years and a new family separating the first from the second and third. But that change from toddler to young girl happened overnight for Neil, Jason and Andrew. 'They're getting towards the end of primary school and if they're not the girls who are dressing and looking sassy, they have friends like that and they see it happening,' Neil says.

A unanimity envelops how fathers see their daughters. Repeatedly, they told stories of tiny princesses who became their little mate, who later developed enormous confidence but still wanted to stay close to their dad. And then, fathers say, they woke up to a new challenge: a tweenie or an adolescent with an independent streak who felt she didn't need him anymore. That happened as her circle of influence grew beyond her family to include other children and their families. Dad's rules, she discovered, were different from the rules enacted in the home of her best friend. Different values come into play too. Girls now know that not everyone thinks like Mum and Dad, and that raises questions in her head. Fathers (and mothers) stop being giants in their world, and they are no longer unchallengeable. Girls learn quickly at school to question statements and challenge claims, and they naturally put that to the test at home.

Most fathers feel that turning point, at middle school, and grapple with their role in dealing with it. 'The saddest day of my life was the day I went to hold her hand, as I had done every morning on the way to school, and she pushed it away,' Colin says. 'I remember it like it was yesterday.' 'If you're doing your job properly as a parent, you're teaching them to challenge things and ask questions,' another father explains. 'And that's what you want them to learn at school, too. But inevitably that means they challenge you and ask questions of you.' It's also at this time that fathers notice changes to their daughters' bodies. They are taking on a new shape, as hormones flare and mood swings set the tone at home. They find their daughters are also less communicative with them. They're now happier in their room – with the door closed – than they are jumping on the trampoline with them.

At this point, many, many fathers see themselves as no longer crucial to their daughters' daily lives. School takes up a big chunk of their day, and technology allows them to continue communicating with their friends long after the school bell stops ringing. It's here, with their daughter about to disappear down the tunnel of teenagehood, and helped by her indifference in some cases and refusal to engage in others, that fathers often find it easier to take a step back. Doing so mutes the never-ending arguments and provides peace for the rest of the family. 'As a father, that's the point where you really want to say, "Well, it's time for Mum to take over. She's the one to deal with this",' Neil says with an honesty and pragmatism born of raising daughters over two generations. 'But you can't pull away like that, because if you do you're out for a long time, aren't you?'

That point is spot on, and if fathers want evidence of it, the girls provide it. When the worst of the teenage storm has passed, at fifteen and sixteen, and seventeen and even eighteen in some cases, girls are not sure how but are desperate to reconnect. Fathers don't know how to do it either. Jess's father is a case in point. She's seventeen. Her father was her everything until Year 8, when she turned more to her mother. She talked to him, over the next few years, but didn't do much with him. She shopped with her mum, and relied on her tutor to help with the homework. He worked hard and supported the family. And now he was offering to teach her to drive. The long hours in the car together would be an antidote to the distance that had grown over the previous few years. But she told him she didn't want him to teach her; she'd ask her brother instead.

Maggie Dent, author and parenting expert, sees how a father's decision to step back takes a toll on girls. 'As soon as puberty hits and they are starting to turn into a woman and they're not a little girl, dads are really mindful that they don't hug them inappropriately and embarrass them or they are called slimy, so they quite often step back physically,' she says. 'Girls have sobbed about that; it can break their heart.' She says that, too often, girls eighteen months later wonder why they felt a gap in their life. 'It's my dad,' they'll conclude.

Almost 400 fathers were either surveyed or interviewed for this book, and you can hear the anguish in their answers when they reveal how they see their relationship with their daughters.

'It was amazing – 10/10 – until she was a teenager. Then the wall came up. I would say it's a work in progress but happy to score it a 7/10.'

'It is trying. We have our good moments, but most of the time I feel like she is questioning me, questioning my authority and direction. I think she thinks she knows better.'

'At fourteen, very good one day a week. The rest not so good. Apparently I don't understand anything – whatever that means!'

'Very close, but she is starting to become more private with her thoughts and activities.'

'Semi-detached at the moment. She is interested in her friends and her own world far more than her family.'

'Had a positive trusting relationship until she turned twelve. Still some moments of affection from her, but she is starting to distance herself from me.'

'Jeez, this is a moment-to-moment proposition. On balance I describe my relationship with my daughter as strong or good. We talk a fair bit and I'm genuinely interested in what's going on for her. She often messages me with quirky good photos or things that have caught her attention. When she is calm she seems to understand my reasons if I've felt the need to apply limits, but in the middle of a meltdown there is no logic or reason.'

'Challenging and sometimes strained. She has been distant and finds it difficult to strike up a good conversation. Often answers are in one or two words.'

Those answers come from fathers whose daughters are aged between twelve and sixteen. The fathers are aged between thirty-eight and sixty-six. Age is relevant to the father–daughter equation in two ways. Firstly, the girls' ages will hint at the trajectory the father–daughter relationship might follow. At eight, fathers know they are unchallenged. That's turned on its head by twelve. At sixteen, fathers hope their daughter has returned – but so much hangs on that, as the following chapters detail. Of course, these are generalisations. Some girls ride through adolescence with their father right next to them. Others, through separation, divorce, illness or death, don't have a father. Others stay by his side until fifteen and then go through a taxing stage. That's one side of the age story, but it is characterised by the cosmic changes brought on by adolescence. The other side of the story relates to a father's age. In this survey, fathers' ages ranged, as already said, from thirty-eight to sixty-six, with most aged forty-three to fifty-five. That means the thirty-eight-year-old might have had his daughter when he was twenty-five; the sixty-six-year-old at fifty-four. These differences don't currently seem to matter: technological challenges, political views and social mores depend more on personality and upbringing than they do on age. But this may change. A quick survey of a dozen thirty-year-old fathers shows them all on Instagram and half of them on Snapchat – although they use it to a lesser extent than their female partners. It is more than plausible, then, that as their children become teens, they will be well versed in social media communication. However, social researcher Mark McCrindle says the average age of a new father now is 33.1 years, and older fathers are becoming a socially acceptable cohort. (Indeed, as their children age this is more likely to affect fathers, not daughters, because they will be extending their active years of parenting.) The other factor with fathers is how anchored their lives are compared to their daughters' over the same period.

While daughters' interests, beliefs, friends and education all change between ages four and fourteen, along with her brain and body, her father's remains fairly steady. He might belong to the same cycling group, hold the same political views and have changed his car only once. He sees his daughter pushing away, and admits it can be testing.

'I would love to be closer and more in the detail sometimes, or make a bigger deal of their successes, but I value their independence more so I back off sometimes and that maybe doesn't encourage them to approach me.'

'Challenging! She is sensitive but very strong-willed. Helping her understand some elements of life is a journey of a million steps.'

'I'm 2IC [second-in-command] *to Mum. I am there for when Mum is not on the scene. We have a nice relationship, but at her age, Mum is the go-to.'*

Exceptions to these comments come, predominantly, from fathers whose daughters are heavily involved in gender-neutral sports like swimming, hockey, soccer, horse-riding, etc. In those cases, fathers see that joint interest as a bond that allows banter and talk to flourish as their daughters grow. And no doubt it is helped by the long hours spent driving to and from practice, games and competitions. The confines of the car – where no-one can escape and daughter and Dad are not looking directly at each other – can encourage some fabulous chats.

But on a day-to-day basis, fathers find those talks difficult. And that means they are not as knowledgeable as they once were about their daughters' activities. Fathers say they no longer understand what their daughters are thinking or feeling. They're not sure whether they're interested in boys or struggling in History or talking to the wrong person on social media. (Just a perspective on the girls here: they miss out too because they are no longer accessing their father's views on different situations. That is crucial – because not only do the more views a girl hears help her formulate her own, but her father is the key to how she sees and relates to other males.) Fathers were asked to nominate the last time they sat down with their daughter, one-on-one, and talked for at least ten minutes.

'A couple of months ago.'

'About a year ago.'

'This month while on holidays.'

'Good question. It's been a while now. Thinking about it now, most if not all of our conversations seem to be built around an issue, a problem, a life lesson, a positive reinforcement, etc. Needs to be some more "just shooting the breeze".'

'*Weeks, not months.*'

'*Good question – probably a few months ago. She is absorbed by her study or other activities.*'

'*Last week we had a good conversation over table tennis for about fifteen minutes.*'

'*A solid ten minutes? Wow, is that still possible?*'

'*Can't remember.*'

'*Often, but my wife talks about the hard stuff.*'

Those fathers who did succeed in spending solid conversational time with their daughters often did it while undertaking specific activities – like sport, or homework, or travelling in the car.

> '*I have found the best way to do this is one-on-one, and in particular when you have them captive in the car (even better when they are learning to drive and have some hours under their belt).*'

> '*Walking the dog together is great because there's no phones.*'

The frankness and forthrightness of fathers is striking. Many say they don't talk very much to their daughters because they don't know what to say, or they're uncertain how their daughter will take it. 'They back off because it's an unknown territory,' Angela White, the executive officer of Adolescent Success, says. 'They don't want to say the wrong thing and they don't want to do the wrong thing either, so it's better just to do nothing,' she adds. Some fathers say they do this out of respect for their daughter; that she deserves both privacy and space. That's true. But it doesn't mean opting out altogether. Angela White gives the positive example of one father who penned a card and left a bunch of flowers on the table during the week his daughter first got her period. 'That was it. For her, it was a really important acknowledgement of the fact that something was happening.' In some homes, prepubescent girls are encouraged to tell their fathers when they first menstruate, and fathers are urged to check that sanitary items are included on weekly grocery lists. A talk my two daughters attended urged girls to demand their dad buy them a new dress when they first got their period! That made it easier for them to raise the issue with their father. The point is that however it is dealt with, it shouldn't be hidden or ignored, because that creates another gap in the father–daughter relationship. 'It's not easy to navigate at all,' Angela White says. 'I reckon it's a balance for the dads – between acknowledging that things are going on without saying the wrong thing.'

Most men struggle to understand how adult women think, and now their 'little mate' is turning out to be just as confusing. (Some fathers see their daughter as a mirror image of their mother.) She is often trying to grapple with this – and will seek independence from her mother in the search for her own identity. Some fathers use their daughter's discomfort as an excuse to distance himself from her at the very time when approval of her is the most important thing. This is what Marise McConaghy, the principal of Strathcona Baptist Girls Grammar School in Melbourne, tells the fathers of students. 'She will be inclined to judge herself harshly. This turning-into-a-woman thing is not working if you, the most important male in her life, have turned away.' Just to make matters more complex, teen boys will become a feature of a girl's life around this time, and some girls might even be experimenting with sexual activity. Some girls may also become attracted to someone of their own gender. If a girl doesn't get approval from her father, she is at risk of seeking that approval elsewhere. Maggie Dent says fathers need to really value how they could help their daughters understand relationships. Good dads, she said, ran the risk of girls believing all men might be kind or principled. 'Most men are good men and we need to tell her that, but some girls are so trusting that they assume all men are going to be just like their dad. So I think it's about making them aware in different situations that not all men are safe and good and can be trusted – and not to be silent if that happens.' It's important, too, that girls have a balanced view of their fathers, and understand their flaws. Psychologist and author Andrew Fuller says he's seen women who have torn up relationship after relationship because every partner fails to live up to the vision they have of their father. 'It's important to have a balanced view of your dad. He's not a superhero. He's a human with all the flaws we all have.'

Fathers describe their daughters' adolescence as an 'awkward' time. 'Walking on eggshells.' 'Not wanting to stuff up.' Their frankness about taking a step back is seen by their daughters' teachers, too. Mum will do the talking, particularly if the matter is personal. Dads will be relegated – or relegate themselves – to a silent supportive role. Toni Riordan, the principal of St Aidan's Anglican Girls' School in Brisbane, says she sees it sometimes at graduation: fathers who are brimming with happiness and pride for their daughters but who stand back and don't involve themselves in the same way as mothers. 'They're so excited to be there with their girls, but they're not the ones receiving all the hugs from the girls. They're there, they're watching, they're just as excited as the mums, but they're not physically as close or present.' Why does she think that's the case? 'Because they're different. They unconsciously know what it's like to be a seventeen-year-old boy. They've grown up slapping boys on the back and punching them in the arm and they don't know that it's okay to hug and cry and squeal and scream.'

Often fathers are also threatened by the independence their daughters show. They shouldn't be. Experts say this independence – and the push for it – is beneficial, and should be viewed that way by fathers. 'We see it in schools,' says Dr Julie Wilson Reynolds, principal of St Hilda's School on Queensland's Gold Coast. 'The parents are here and the girls are doting on their parents, and then there's less or more careful involvement – a stage in adolescence where girls and parents negotiate with each other about boundaries.' But she says that rather than view it with disappointment, fathers should see it as a daughter's rite of passage and a positive realignment of not just loyalty but of independence, of self-efficacy, of knowing their daughter is able to make decisions for herself.

Fathers say their confidence can take a pounding, too. 'They get to a point where they are better than us at something – whether it's technology or sport,' one father of a thirteen-year-old and fourteen-year-old says. The girls admit, too, that they can become harsh and dismissive of their father and his views, as they seek less protection and more self-reliance. 'When they are tiny it's just so easy,' Neil says. 'It's clear what fatherhood is. Whatever the situation, we can just pick them up and take them away from danger. But as they get older, we even lose the ability to physically do that!'

Tim has three daughters, aged fifteen, thirteen and eleven, and he loves every moment of being a dad. Well, most moments. He sees having daughters as easier than having sons, because girls are not prone to injuries in the same way as boys, and take considerably fewer risks. But he knows there's a flip side he needs to consider, too, and this year's #metoo campaign brought that home. Several of the men I interviewed said the knowledge of what was happening in workplaces – and that their daughters could fall victim to it – horrified them. If it had happened to so many other young women, how could they ensure it did not happen to their own daughters? Tim says he used it as a platform to tell his daughters not to take everyone at face value.

Ross's daughters straddle in age the spectrum through which fathers see their daughters travel from eleven to sixteen. At eleven, he says, his experience tells him that girls can become very upset very quickly. 'Everything is really big. Things become very tearful. Anything that goes wrong is a major disaster,' he says. His youngest daughter is illustrating that textbook behaviour now. But his thirteen-year-old is through that. She's in the 'cool' stage. 'At thirteen, it's like, "whatever",' he says. She's less fazed about schedule changes or events that would have sent her running to her room in tears only a year or two earlier. His fifteen-year-old, he says, is finding 'reason' once again. 'By fifteen they have a bit more control of their lives, or know perhaps where they are headed.' Of course, that's not always the case, but a four-year period in this one family shows the enormous breadth and variation of empathy fathers need to have to help their daughters. Mothers often understand this more readily because they have travelled the same path; they can remember turning eleven and thirteen and fifteen. Ross says he's taken to using humour to deal with the highs and the lows, and mimics his daughters constantly. (The target, he says, never finds it amusing – but her siblings always do.)

Ross's case also shows that no two daughters are the same, and fathers' handling of situations needs to mirror that. He says, for example, that his daughters learn in entirely different ways. 'The oldest one is very auditory. The youngest is like me: she learns by doing things. And the middle one is very visual. So there are different ways of trying to teach them things. They click with a teacher who teaches them that way better than another way,' he says. Knowing the strengths of each child has helped deepen his relationship with them.

This, surely, is a textbook case for 'agile parenting'. Catherine O'Kane, who heads All Hallows' School in Brisbane, says parenting has changed considerably over the past generation and that needs to be reflected in dealings with our own children. 'We can't think the parenting we learnt as children from the example of our parents is actually going to set us up for the children of today, because the world is so different,' she says. It isn't an issue of changing values but in ensuring that connections, built on understanding, stay alive. 'The idea of changing your mind about what is good parenting is something that modern parents need to have in spades,' Catherine O'Kane says. Diana Vernon, from Melbourne's Methodist Ladies' College, says a father needs to remember that 'his relationship has got to change with his daughter because she is going through such tremendous change'. She continues: 'It's just recognising that your little girl is going to change – and by the way, she's changing far more dramatically than you are.' It is crucial, she says, to listen and 'be there' for them. 'When people look for houses it's location, location, location. With parenting it's listening, listening, listening. Being there, being there, being there.'

Dr Briony Scott, the principal of Wenona – a day and boarding school for girls from Kindergarten to Year 12 – in Sydney, says fathers need to move from issuing instructions to a young child, to helping them, in their teens, understand why he takes that position. 'Then it goes both ways,' she says. 'You do have to listen to them. Young people are clever, but not wise. Treating them like fools doesn't help; it just gets their back up. What they don't have is wisdom, so you want to help them and listen to them.' She says that from the age of thirteen, all students at Wenona are treated as young women. 'Now, they may act like children from time to time, but I treat them and speak to them like they are women because that's what they respond to. They listen more if they are spoken to respectfully and if their opinions are heard.' Dr Scott says thumping the table never works. And almost every expert agrees that removing a mobile phone as punishment doesn't work either.

In looking at how fathers see their daughters, one final issue needs to be canvassed. Children are maturing more quickly because they are exposed to a greater number of influences, and as parents we are more attuned to risks that were not obvious twenty-five years ago. One of those threats relates to the coverage of sexual abuse, and the chance that it can lead to wrongful accusations. When I first heard this from fathers, I was flabbergasted. But it is real: it is the reason some men will not teach; it is the reason some fathers will not follow their daughters on Instagram; it is the reason why a father might not allow his ten-year-old daughter to go for a sleepover at a friend's home. It is also the reason why some fathers will not allow groups of his daughters' friends to sit around at his home without a female adult present. 'One thing I'd say as a father of daughters is that I'm more reluctant to be in charge of a group of girls than I was twenty-five years ago,' Neil says. 'Things can be misconstrued, and I think everything we've come to learn over the past twenty-five years about the bad things that have happened in the world – especially sex offences relating to kids – means you do run a little risk, if you are alone with girls, of something being misconstrued. Maybe you pick up a kid, or pick them up in the wrong way, and the next thing that child might tell their parents and you are being put in the category of having to defend yourself.' Girls miss out there, too. One seventeen-year-old explained that she'd never had a birthday party, because she lived with her father, who was single. He was not going to play host to a big group of teenage girls. 'He said it wasn't right – so I missed out,' she says.

If there is a message in how fathers see their daughters, Dr Briony Scott sums it up beautifully. She says that what a girl thinks of herself almost matches up with what she thinks her father thinks of her – not what he thinks but what she *perceives* he thinks. 'If they see the back of someone as they're walking away, that's a pretty clear message,' she says. 'It might not be what is happening, but what we do know is that young people are very, very bad at ascribing meaning to actions.' They can be egocentric and over-personalise things. 'So if they see Dad walking away it means far more to them than it would to us as an adult,' she says. Fathers might see their daughters becoming difficult to deal with; 'stepping back' is not the answer.

4

How daughters see their dads

Lucy is holding centre stage, the tree's canopy providing refuge from the midday sun in the middle of the school ground. Her friends – all fourteen and fifteen – are doubled over laughing as they announce what they believe their father would buy them if entrusted to go clothes shopping. Lucy does not hesitate: 'A pair of shorts with unicorns on them.' She belly laughs, like it's the funniest thing she's ever heard. Emily joins in: 'Not ripped jeans, that's for sure!' Annie waits her turn: 'Something he's seen me wear, because then he'd think there was more of a chance I'd like it!' Kate hangs back. 'I wouldn't know,' she says. And she doesn't want to find out. 'I wouldn't trust him with it.' Hannah takes what seems like minutes to come up with her answer, egged on by her friends to be honest. 'Something sport-related,' the swimmer says. 'Probably *another* pair of togs.'

The message is clear: dads don't have a clue about fashion. It wasn't only because styles changed so regularly, or that they were now largely responsible for their own fashion choices. Nor did they attribute their father's lack of knowledge about their dress sense to the fact that traditionally it hasn't been a dad's job to buy his teen's wardrobe. These girls, when pressed, believed their dads did not know them well enough.

This is central to how girls see their fathers. Of course there are exceptions, but the vast majority believe their fathers do not really know them – and that they know them less as they grow older. As little girls, they could all recall their father reading to them and knowing their favourite songs by heart. Their dad knew their favourite colour and their favourite ice-cream flavour, too. He was fun with a capital F. He defended her, played with her and always took her side. But then, around the age of eleven or twelve, things changed. The girls I spoke to admitted that maybe they stopped being as open with him, but he didn't try like he used to, either. By thirteen or fourteen, these girls say the chasm in their relationship was, on some days, insurmountable.

Many are unperturbed by that; it was 'awkward' for Dad to know too much about them now. They didn't want him asking about their friends or what they were doing on Instagram. But many others were desperate to revive the relationship they had, and didn't know where to start. They wanted to go back to 'doing things' with their father, activities varying from going to the movies to going camping. But how do they go about asking?

From the girls' answers it was apparent that the perceived 'separation' between father and daughter had a range of causes. Her father's long working hours, or working away, a natural closeness to her mother, circumstance, a belief that her father was no longer as interested in her and didn't know how to communicate with her, all played a role in girls' perceptions that their father now didn't know them as well as their mother, siblings, friends and, in many cases, even teachers. Technology and her father's age – irrespective of whether he was thirty-eight or sixty-six – were also catalysts for girls seeing the bond with their father as superficial. Take these answers to the question *Does your father understand your life?*

'No. He's old.'

'No. Yesterday Mum and I were talking about rowing and he did not know which club I was allowed to row *for, when Mum and I have been talking about it for the past six months!'*

'He does, but I don't think any dad will ever truly understand the pressures that occur among teenage girls.'

'No, because he hates technology but doesn't understand that it's always been a big part of my life.'

'No, I don't think he does. He missed a whole chunk of it and still isn't there for all of it now. He doesn't understand how serious I am about playing netball in the future, doesn't understand that I want to go to uni, doesn't understand that I get upset over things in my life sometimes and sometimes I don't need him to fix it. I just need him to listen.'

Background was cited as one of the reasons he was unable to understand her. There's a strapping irony here. Many of these girls' fathers grew up poor, or as immigrants, or the children of immigrants. They lived on the land during punishing times, or in homes that hugged the outer edges of big cities where freedom was large but grandeur small. But through their hard work and sacrifice they gifted their daughters a childhood they never had. Annual holidays. Dance lessons. Birthday parties each year. Now, though, many girls see that as a reason their father doesn't get the hang of their lives. 'My childhood is completely different to his,' Ruby says. 'He grew up in a poor family on a farm, while I am being raised in a middle-class family in the city. There's also a generation and culture gap with regards to study and life.' Sandy says: 'He would understand parts of my life, but he isn't the one who's a fifteen-year-old girl in the 21st century. He's a fifty-three-year-old man born into a Catholic Italian family in the '60s. He cannot understand tech for the life of him, so I help him. It's stuff like that.' This may be unfair to those fathers, but it is how their daughters see things. To others, Dad is also a Luddite in an age where technology is like oxygen, where Instagram is the lifeblood of their friendship groups, where clothes are bought online and where Netflix is watched at convenience. That isn't all bad; their fathers' lack of knowledge around Snapchat and Instagram in some ways serves as a blessing. 'The less Dad knows, the better,' one girl quipped. Several others explained that they saw their father's interest in social media revolving around data, fees, insurance policies and broken screens – not *how* they were using it.

Unsurprisingly, a strong concordance arises when the girls nominate the character traits they'd like to change in their fathers. For teens, they are fathers treating them 'like little girls' or 'not letting me grow up', not 'taking me seriously and listening to me'. The age gap between father and daughter means, for many of them, that it is almost impossible for their fathers to grasp the complexity of being a teen. 'He doesn't understand what it is like to be a teenager in today's society, as it requires a lot of effort to fit in and to develop those great friendships in high school,' Mary says. And his age means the world has moved on from the pre-smartphone 'old days' when their fathers swam in the local creek, without permission, and spent most of their waking hours outside of their homes. 'He doesn't know what it is like to be a teenage girl growing up in this world of social media and going to an all-girls school and all the pressure put on us by our parents, friends and teachers,' another says. Girls say this lack of understanding informs his opinions on topics ranging from same-sex marriage to republicanism, from equal pay to the treatment of refugees.

A flip side exists to all of this, for while hundreds of girls saw their fathers' outdated views or inability to use technology in the way they did as an impediment to their relationship, hundreds of others believed their father did – or tried to – comprehend a teenage life alien to his own. They also applauded their father for being less judgemental than their mother, and this surfaced time and time again. This is a piece of gold that fathers need to exploit, because their daughters' vulnerability means every passing judgement can cut to the core. Often, girls do not want their problem fixed; they just want to be heard. A sturdy correlation also exists between those girls who see their father as understanding their lives and those who believe their fathers listen to them.

Girls' views of their fathers change, and become more sophisticated, as they travel through their teens. Younger girls label their fathers as funny and inspirational, brave and sensible. They love their calmness and believe their musical taste trumps their mothers'. Asked to nominate what they loved about their dads, younger girls were delightfully literal. He was 'big and brave', or had a 'comfy tummy' or 'nice dark hair'. He tanned in summer, and ate fast food. But those views become more complex once the girls reach the age of twelve or thirteen, when their answers span humour, attitude, intelligence, hard work and reason.

> 'His attitude towards helping me in challenging situations. I was upset after not doing well in a lesson. Mum asks why I didn't do well. Dad hugs me.'

> 'Hardworking, caring, a unique sense of humour, one where play wrestling becomes a thing in our kitchen.'

> 'He is very hardworking and dedicated. He never ever starts something and doesn't finish.'

> 'He has brains and business skills and a positive attitude.'

Persistence, work ethic, confidence and intelligence rated the most highly, followed closely by drive, his easy manner, being non-judgemental, being logical, organised, smart, and staying calm when bedlam explodes around him. Not overdramatising things, tenaciousness – these are a father's best attributes, according to his daughters. And while they don't use the word resilience, that seems to be what they're describing. 'He keeps going, no matter what,' one said. He is able to bounce back. To see the flip side of a bad situation. To not think a tiny problem will end the world. To calmly find a solution. These attributes – nominated by the girls – match almost precisely those traits experts say our girls need. And that makes a father's role in passing them on all the more crucial.

'He had a very unsettling and negative upbringing and I admire the way that he has bounced back from that, and strived in every possible way to make my upbringing unlike his,' Lilli says. And Sara says: 'He has come from absolutely nothing. He immigrated to have a better life from Africa. He is passionate and hardworking and ambitious.' Kate says this: 'I admire his ability to see the logic in everything. I remember being upset over finding it hard to make new friends when I moved schools, and when I could not be comforted by my mother I rang my father. He gave me a huge reality check and reminded me of all the facts – I had only been there for three weeks and I couldn't expect to adjust to the school so soon. He told me it would take time, but that it would happen eventually. His logic made sense to me and I felt a lot better.' Kate is one girl, but many others described similar circumstances when Dad used logic over emotion, and recalled the comfort that that provided. Many others saw their father as the inspiration when a problem surfaced and they needed to find a way around it. For a cohort whose days are so often enveloped by emotion and drama, Dad's logic or reason is a wonderful antidote.

Educators see the change in how girls consider their fathers as they travel through middle school and into senior school. It's normal for teenagers to separate from their parents at this point, but principal Toni Riordan offers an interesting reflection here. 'I don't think they let go of Dad as quickly as they let go of Mum, probably because Dad is standing back anyway,' she says. That feeds the view that often it is fathers, rather than daughters, who take the first step back. But usually, in their senior years, girls become hungry for adult interaction and start to develop their views and refine their opinions based on those expressed by parents, teachers and others. As said before, it's clear that those dads who refuse to step back during adolescence – despite being regularly shunned by their daughters – are more readily sought out at this point. Their daughters know they've been there, they feel secure and loved, and it's at this point that many of them turn back towards their fathers.

One last compelling insight here, in looking at how girls see their fathers. When they are young, their fathers are hilarious. 'Dad tells the best jokes,' one says. 'My dad is very funny and has a whole lot of jokes that make me laugh,' another says. 'Dad has more jokes than anyone in the world,' according to a third. These girls are in Year Five, but here's a hint: it's unlikely they will repeat those statements at thirteen, when the comedy routine can quickly be seen as a torment. The joker card has an expiry date, and it's worth every dad learning when the line has been crossed.

What do you call a fake noodle? An impasta.

What do you get if you cross a parrot with a centipede? A walkie-talkie.

Why did the boy take a ruler to bed with him? Because he wanted to see how long he slept.

What did the traffic light say to the zebra crossing? Don't look now, I'm changing.

Across the country, girls can parrot their dad's favourite joke. 'When we are having pasta, Dad says, "I taught Aleni to dance",' Shelley says. 'Dad will say, "Nice trip. I'll see you next fall,"' her friend quips. 'And it wasn't funny the first time.' It's fair to say that girls' definition of 'funny' changes rapidly with the onset of adolescence, where Dad's jokes, straight out of a Christmas bon-bon pack, turn 'lame', 'daggy' and 'embarrassing'. This can be hard for fathers to understand, because their jokes haven't changed; their daughters have. Furthermore, the line between 'funny' and 'teasing' is blurry, and can be restyled on a daily basis. Humour can be a green card or a red card to fathers. It's wonderful to make them laugh or have their eyes roll in mock despair, but when it leans towards teasing, the girls switch off. I didn't find an exception to that statement, in any school, in any town or city, in any state. Jokes are not personal. Teasing, however, targets a vulnerability that sends them to their room. Young girls see jokes as easy banter with their dad, and older girls will laugh off impersonal jokes as 'Dad being Dad'. Indeed, the jokes serve their purpose when a girl rolls her eyes; it's a healthy sign. But if they can construe (or misconstrue) them as reflecting on them, the joke becomes a verdict. They see it as a judgement by their fathers: he's telling them what he thinks.

'I was so hurt when I finally came home with an academic award,' Abby says. 'Dad said I should take it back to school and see if there had been a mix-up in the names. I know to him it was a joke, but he turned the thing I was most proud of into something that was a joke. I went to bed and cried.' Abby's sensitivity to her father's clumsy joke is mirrored widely. Trinity is a boarder and says she feels as though her father can't ever show pride in her achievements. 'He grew up – he's Italian – having a hard life and being tested a lot. But now when I ring and say "Hey Dad, I got an academic award," he says, "Why you? That doesn't sound right."' Tears are moments away. She knows he's trying to be funny, but it just doesn't cut it. Beth Oakley, Wenona's deputy principal (student wellbeing) says fathers can underestimate their daughters' fragility to throwaway lines. 'A comment from Dad will carry more weight than so much. She'll hold it – and he may not even notice it,' she says. 'An older and more robust girl, would say "Gee thanks, Dad," and he'd say, "You know what I mean; I'm so proud of you" and it would have moved on quickly.' Another principal tells the story of watching television with her husband when their teen daughter appeared, dressed to go to a party. 'Are you going to a fancy dress party, darling,' he ventured. The daughter stamped off in a huff. Twenty minutes later, their second daughter appeared. She was dressed in a very short dress, with six-centimetre heels. 'I just put my finger up to his mouth so he didn't say a word,' said the principal. He thought her dress was inappropriate. She agreed, but with a pragmatism born of educating young women told him not to worry. 'It will last about five minutes,' she told him. 'And sure enough,' she says now, 'we have one of the most conservative girls.'

So, just for the record, jeans that are ripped don't need mending, and the hairdresser knew the dye was purple before using it. A teenage girl just wants to be taken seriously, and any joke directed at her appearance or talent is likely to fail. This shouldn't come as a surprise to fathers. Men are unlikely to poke fun at their partner's appearance or intelligence, so why would a vulnerable girl, on the brink of womanhood, find it amusing? A checklist here is hardly needed, but just in case: hair, make-up, clothing, weight, mood swings, menstruation, body hair and sexuality should be off any joke lists. One of the girls put it this way, when asked what she'd like to tell her father: 'You may think that what you say to me will not leave a lasting imprint, but I value your opinion more than anyone's. When you tease me or make mean jokes about the things I am most proud of, it hurts and that's what I remember most vividly.' She values his opinion, more than anyone's. Experts back this up: Dad's opinion is absolutely crucial to girls, whether they are aged six or seventeen.

Tom Matthews says that in the mire of adolescence, teenagers are not always good at reading intentions, and he knew from experience how his own daughter could interpret something very differently from what he meant. 'I think there are times when we can joke to defuse an argument – when what our teenagers hear and want is just to be listened to and understood,' he says. He says that when girls are most needy they can be at their most 'obnoxious'. 'When they're the most obnoxious we want to lecture or we want to joke ...' But that's not a good idea. His advice? Fathers should stop and listen to the language their daughters are speaking. They might then not proceed with the joke. David Smith, the principal of Calrossy Anglican School in Tamworth, is with the girls on this score. He says he learnt how jokes can go awry the hard way, raising three daughters. 'I'll put my hand up and say I've been very guilty at times of being very insensitive to the girls. So I actually think dads need to learn – and my girls said that.' Smith says girls will, every now and again, let their fathers know how they are feeling, but it was easy to miss if they weren't listening hard. 'One of the big lessons for each dad is that it's different for each child and your relationship is different with each,' he says.

Girls want their fathers to be non-judgemental. They want them to listen to what they are struggling to tell them. They truly value their opinion, even when they pretend they don't, and they want to keep the flame of that bond, developed even before they could climb up on their father's knee, alive. So what does she really want from her father? And how does she go about asking for that?

5

What she really wants (and needs)

Gracie, twelve, is hiding in her room. She's spent a taxing day at school and she's just heard her father's car pull into the garage. He's the last person she wants to see. Why? Her period had begun that day, just before recess. She'd worried about who she should tell through to lunchtime, and then her friend took her to the school nurse. A change of uniform and she was fine. Telling her mum after school was easy. She had given her a big hug and a cup of hot chocolate. But Dad? He didn't need to know; she didn't want him to know; it was none of his business anyway! Her mother knocked on the door and coaxed her downstairs. 'Don't tell him, Mum!' she pleaded. 'I already have, sweetie; it's fine,' she responded.

What Gracie's father says next is vital. A sentence, a few words – that's all it takes to signal to his daughter that he accepts that she is growing up. In this instance, Gracie's father is not too sure of what to say. He knows he shouldn't make a joke of it, despite that being his default position. But he's not too keen to get into a big conversation about it. Wouldn't it be easier if his wife dealt with it?

Acknowledging that a girl is growing up is one of the best things a father can do for his daughter, according to Adolescent Success's Angela White. And that moment when a daughter becomes an adult – or learns about sex or confronts an adult issue for the first time – can be a moment where father and daughter bond . . . or separate. 'Some girls coast through adolescence, and you wouldn't even know they're going through anything,' she says. 'But other girls really struggle with it. And for their dad, it's almost a secret thing. A girl gets her period. The men in the house don't know about it. So then there's a sudden change in the relationship with her father – and there's this side of her she's keeping from him.' White says no big discussion is needed; just an 'acceptance from Dad' that his daughter is growing up. Still, she says, fathers routinely struggle with that. 'An in-tune dad is going to pick up pretty quickly when his daughter's body is changing and she's suddenly shyer – and that causes him to back off.' He wants to provide privacy, or he might be unsure what to say or how to say it. But families need to make room in the discussion for fathers, she says, and a simple acknowledgement – a 'congratulations' – could provide his daughter with a sound pillar of support.

So what does a teen girl really want, and need, from her father? How can he help her to navigate those crucial years while building the bond they've both treasured? If you were doing a wall planner of the ways fathers could help, you'd pick a mighty-sized wall. Researchers, school educators, academics, school counsellors, parenting experts and psychologists credit fathers with a long list of potential attributes that can help their daughters. Building confidence, providing a can-do attitude, gifting her an ability to stand up and be heard (whether it's on drugs, sex or a political issue), encouraging learning and injecting a dose of perspective are all wonderful attributes she can learn from a male role model in her life. So are the ability to set goals, grow in independence, learn how she should be treated by men, value being honest and acquire the understanding that an apology doesn't signal a weakness. Practical things feature strongly, too, like learning to drive, changing a tyre, replacing a light bulb, understanding the weather system, and the finer tips of AFL. These can be taught by people other than a girl's father – including her mother – but instruction in them can provide fathers with an opportunity to stay close to their daughters.

Girls, even if they don't show it, want their fathers to remain part of their lives. In interviews across the country, this was a key message. Of course, some girls articulated the opposite, telling of fathers who they believed had deserted them and their mother, fathers who were more interested in their brothers, fathers who spent days away from the family, or were violent, or lived under the same roof but with no emotional stake in what happened to the family. But the vast majority of girls could detail what they would like their father to do to improve their relationship, and how their father could help them.

'Be there more.'

'Put the phone away and not just focus on the solution. Talk about it.'

'While he's present at home a lot, he's not always mentally present, and sometimes when I need him to focus on something that has to do with me, he doesn't. This is especially frustrating if I've created something for him that may take a bit of effort to look at and he tells me he'll get to it later and never does.'

'Spend more time with me.'

'More time surfing and talking together.'

'Maybe be around a bit more and could eat dinner with the rest of the family more often.'

'He needs to spend more time with the family and less time working.'

'He is constantly travelling and is not often home, but that is because of work so I am understanding of it. We could also have more family dinners together because he usually isn't at the table for very long.'

After 'being there', doing things together features strongly.

'Play with me.'

'My dad has problems with his knees so he can't do much activity but we used to go out and play volleyball. I loved it so much. For five years he hasn't been allowed to but I wish he could.'

'I would like to go camping once.'

'He could get involved in some more activities I enjoy and understand why I like them.'

'Support me more by going to more of my extracurricular activities.'

'He could take me out for a walk or a bike ride or something.'

'My father could be available for me on the weekends to play a board game or cards or a video game.'

'My dad is super competitive. I'm super competitive. I'd love to go go-kart racing. It would be so cool. But it costs a lot of money.'

'He always puts in an effort, but to extend an effort he could maybe offer to take me somewhere we both like.'

'I'd love to do the Kokoda Track with Dad. Dad would love that. He'd find it a real challenge and I'd love to do that with him.'

Curiously, as articulate as they are, and as fiery as they can be, few girls specifically request their father do activities with them. Their reasons are varied, but the most common is a fear that he might say no. Other reasons are that he seems too busy, they don't want to bother him, and it might cost too much money. Parenting expert Maggie Dent says that girls are likely to read a mild 'no' from Dad as a serious rejection. 'It's not for him; he might just be busy – but they stop asking in case they get rejected.' What makes it worse, she says, is that Mum is often able to work out what her daughter wants and girls expect their fathers to be able to do the same. That's why, Dent says, it is so crucial for fathers and daughters to share quiet moments together, and find connections.

One example she gives is of a Perth father who shared a love of AC/DC with his daughter, starting when she was only seven. For years, they'd sing loud, and often out of tune. It was their 'thing'. And then, eventually, they flew across the country for an AC/DC concert. His daughter is unlikely ever to forget that connection forged listening to *Back in Black*, and *Highway to Hell*. Dent says she's never forgotten a particular moment she spent with her own father, as a child. The fifth of six children, she was her father's offsider. 'From very young – under three – I was up and out the door with my dad almost every morning to go in the ute to do farm work – check the sheep, the fences and have morning tea at Granny's,' Dent says. But this one day is indelibly marked in her mind. She was telling her father a story. He turned off the ute's ignition, turned, and listened to her. And she's never forgotten that precious moment. 'My Dad made me "feel felt" – this is a concept that means so much more than the overworked term "loved". When we feel felt by someone, it shapes the way we see ourselves profoundly. My dad gave me my sense that I had value, I was worthwhile, and for that I am eternally grateful.'

Girls state that their fathers acknowledging their efforts, and treating them as young women, is crucial. This is how they responded to the question: *What do you want your dad to do?*

'Understand that I am no longer five.'

'Talk to me as if I am fourteen, not nine.'

'My dad worked so hard for the family that he sometimes forgot to do little things like tell us he loves us or is really proud of our achievements. It's pretty typical of Asian parenting. He upheld education as being important, so I tried to get good marks all my life, but sometimes I didn't feel as appreciated or rewarded as my friends were; instead it was just an expectation of me.'

'More recognition of the good things I do.'

'When he says he's proud, he should show it.'

Experts explain that teens are looking, all the time, for clues their parents love them. They want to know that their father is there and that he's proud of them. Some principals say that parent-anxiety has now reached fever pitch and this is hampering parents taking a balanced approach to raising their children. One says that immediately something goes wrong, the drama dial is ratcheted up. If the school wants to discuss why a child is not doing their homework, a parent might now jump to the conclusion that 'she has gone off the rails and could be headed for a life of drugs or prostitution'. Some parents' response is driven by a fear or an anxiety that saying 'no' to their daughter will mean she walks out of their lives, also.

'So what do girls want from their dad?' Dr Briony Scott is asking – and answering – the question. 'They want to be loved. They want to be accepted. They want an advocate. They want someone they can talk to. They want what any of us wants from people we adore. I don't think dads are that different from mums or any of us, really.'

Of course, a daughter's wants and needs can run to pages, especially if she is drawing up the list. But wanting her father to stop being over-protective, having modern views on feminism, religion and immigration issues, and accepting that boyfriends will be part of their teen journey, were also highly cited. The list of 'wants' were similar whether girls were aged ten or seventeen, although the younger ones' comments were delightful in their specifics. 'Hug me more', 'more daddy–daughter time' and wanting more play time – 'when I ask him to go into the pool now, he says his back is sore' – all featured. Several younger girls also suggested their relationship would improve if their father stopped smoking. In the following chapters, experts explain how fathers might provide those gifts their daughters want . . . and need. Happily, fathers, when asked what they would like, shadowed their daughters' responses. Two answers stood out: having more time to spend with their daughter, and being able to communicate with her.

'I'd like to spend more one-on-one time [with my daughter] – e.g. bush walking or camping.'

'I would like to get back to more one-on-one time with my girls. The last eighteen months have been very difficult with work and it has impacted on the time I used to spend with them.'

'I need to gain an understanding of how she thinks and why she thinks that way to improve it. Also I need to spend more time with her, but in the past six months she's been unwilling and I've only seen her one time. Our relationship is done by text now, and if I didn't text her she would not contact me.'

'I would like to improve my communication with her so that she could come to me about issues. To be more discursive and less shouty.'

'Become better at sharing emotions and feelings with each other. Having her fully comfortable saying what she thinks and what's on her mind, particularly if she thinks it differs to my view or what she thinks I'm thinking.'

'Whilst we have lovely conversations about society, politics, business etc., I'd like our conversations to be more about them personally.'

Fathers saw clear obstacles to this happening, the principal one being separation, for those fathers who lived elsewhere. But other issues also acted as brakes to bonding.

'By remaining patient I'm starting to see the way ahead to again being able to communicate with my daughter without the discussion crumbling into a spate of words we both later regret.'

'I would like to have more time to sit and listen but they would also need to be willing to do the same.'

'I'd like to be able to improve communication ... as a bloke it's difficult to understand when to ask questions versus wait for my daughter to open up.'

No-one says this is an easy course for fathers. Indeed, Julie Feeney, the deputy principal at Mater Christi College in Belgrave, Victoria, says girls' wants and needs might even depend on the day. 'I think a father has to be perceptive, because when things are going well it's straightforward but when there's a friendship fallout or a poor result at school or someone looks at her in a mean way, Dad has to look for the cue in the girls' behaviour,' she says. 'That's hard, because adult males behave very differently to adolescent girls. What makes them tick is different.' She says that if perception fails, fathers should ask their daughter whether things are okay without making it a challenging question. That means going around, rather than straight to, the issue. Instead of asking 'What's the matter?', it might mean asking 'How's your day been?'. It also means looking for changes in a girl's behaviour – removing themselves from the family table, not eating, being listless, and a dramatic change in dress style. Julie Feeney says some changes are inevitable during adolescence. Perhaps they'll take to wearing flannelette shirts and tracksuit pants with holes in them. Does it matter? No! Pick your battles. Experts commonly use terms like 'a minefield' to describe parenting adolescents, because what can be guaranteed one day can be completely off the table the next. That's why perception and intuition and agile parenting are so important. 'The better the father has known the little girl, the more likely he will be to understand her as she grows into adolescence,' Feeney says. Acceptance is also important here, according to experts. This doesn't mean acceptance of bad behaviour, but accepting a teen girl for who she is. Angela White put it this way: 'Girls can feel fine one day and the next day feel snappy or tired. It can have a huge impact on girls as they are growing into womanhood. They're stepping into that adolescence where their bodies are changing, so acceptance of the fact that they might not operate in the same way men do is important.' This too can be hard on fathers, who don't understand the ups and downs of adolescent hormones. A father might never have had a headache. He might get up every Saturday morning and follow the same routine, including mowing the lawn after breakfast. Acceptance means that his daughter might not be able to do that. Some days are diamonds, other days are not.

Pushing a teen girl into a corner, where she feels she has no 'out', can be counterproductive. An example here is a student who stops practising the flute after her parents have paid for lessons, continually, for five years. But at fifteen, can you force her to practise? Is it that she doesn't like the flute? Is it interfering with time she thinks is best put into something else? Or is it that she is playing up? One primary school teacher says this: 'They are expecting their daughters to have resilience and tenacity, to stick with things or put up with things. But how are they teaching that? Do they see a dad who just gets on with things? Or do they sit them down and explain how they deal with frustration, or what they think when things get hard and pass on those lessons?'

Girls understand that they could do more to help cement their relationship with their fathers. They are even able to articulate what they would change to make that bond stronger. Take this example from Sophie, who is fifteen. 'I'd take him on more bike rides and not be embarrassed riding along the street with him. I used to do it, but now it's a bit weird riding along with your dad with a massive helmet on.' Would you do it if he asked? 'Yes!' Why don't you ask him? 'Because . . . I don't know.' Such responses were common. They'd talk to Dad more if he talked to them more. They'd hang out with him more if he showed signs that he wanted to do that too. While the onus is on the adult to lead the relationship, surely girls need to step up here? At school they are taught to speak up, fashion an argument, be bold. Author and psychologist Andrew Fuller says girls' inability to seek out what they want reflects a broad lack of role-modelling of father–daughter relationships. 'I can't think of an example in popular media of a really good father–daughter relationship,' he says.

A few other tips here in terms of what girls want, and how experts believe their fathers can help them. First, admitting fault is good. Experts explain it this way. Everybody gets something wrong, and if in the early years a father can apologise to his daughter for making mistakes, it opens the door for her knowing she can also get something wrong and admit it. It matters less, they say, what any one issue is than actually using the words 'I'm sorry. I got it wrong.' It also demonstrates that no-one is perfect, and lets her know that no-one expects her to be perfect, either. The second issue is consistency, particularly when it comes to storytelling. How many times has a father, standing around the barbecue, talked about the antics he got up to at his daughter's age? From staying out until 2 am, to playing truant and driving before getting his licence, to playing on the roof, to going swimming in the local creek. They make great stories, but they can also signal to their daughter that he did things at her age that he's now not allowing her to do. And his daughter is likely to see that either as her father being over-protective, or sexist. Or both.

Girls want to understand their fathers, as much as their fathers are searching for a how-to manual on teen girls. As part of this research, I asked girls what issue they would like me to research to help them in their relationship with their father. The answers ran to pages and pages, but here is a cross-section of them.

'Why do dads never open up when they are struggling or going through a low point in life, because we can help them too. We are expected to open up about our life struggles, so why don't they? If they open up I would be more inclined to do the same.'

'Is it normal if you don't have a close relationship with your father to seek a different father-figure in your life?'

'Why are daughters more reluctant to talk to their dad than their mum, even if they have a good relationship?'

'Why are fathers so hard on their daughters? Why do fathers feel the need to be so protective of their daughters, not their sons?'

'Try looking into whether the daughter shares the same values as their father and see how that correlates with their relationship.'

'How do I improve Dad's listening?'

'Do they want their daughters to be girly or strong or smart?'

'I personally would love there to be some sort of book or guide for international parents who have children born in Australia to help them realise what it is like and how to communicate with a child in the era of technology.'

'I think you should look into how different society was in the '70s and '80s, as that's when most of our parents were growing up, and it would show how they really have no idea how much harder it is to grow up in today's society, especially being a young girl (with sexism, misogyny and the sexualisation of women).'

'I know it's hard for fathers to discuss feelings and all the sappy stuff, but I know that if my dad would have ever once made the effort to ask if I was okay or if I had any problems going on with my friends, or any questions like that, I would probably still be talking to him today. So I guess if I had two questions they would be, (1) why is it so hard for fathers to discuss their feelings? And (2), do most fathers really know how much just making the effort to discuss problems or things in our lives impacts on our father–daughter relationship?'

The correlation between what girls and fathers want is strong. And that largely matches what experts say are the ingredients of a warm and powerful relationship.

That means the problem is in the 'doing' – finding the time to embark on activities or to talk, and knowing how to communicate with each other. 'Life isn't simple for a twelve- to thirteen-year-old, despite not being obliged to earn a living and comprehend real responsibilities,' Elisabeth says. 'Life can get immensely tough, settling into new schools, finding a friendship group, the pressure of tests, keeping up with your homework, growing up, boys and general bitchiness.'

Sometimes, girls want the simplest of things.

> *'I wish I could talk to him about boys. I wish he would tell me, like they do in cheesy movies, that no-one would ever be good enough for me.'*

> *'If you die, what career would you want me to have and are you proud to be my father?'*

> *'When was the last time you went through a struggling time? What helped? How long did it last?'*

So how does her father start these conversations?

6

He said. She said.

Frank reckons almost everything is working in his house. His only daughter, at twelve, is delightful. She's on the cusp of developing a bit of attitude, but he remembers what he was like and considers himself lucky. 'I always try and do the right thing by her,' he says. 'I do travel a lot, but when I'm home I'm there, and if I say I'm going to be at something I will be there. I try to be really consistent.' But one issue continues to bug him, he tells me, and that relates to how he and his wife communicate with their daughter. His wife jumps in with 'don't pick on her, she is fragile' or takes his daughter's side while he is disciplining her, and he's not sure how to handle that. 'Now I am very cognisant of my daughter changing, however sometimes I find it difficult to balance the "emotional changes" with "Mum's emotions" with "Hey, I know you're emotional but you still have to clean up after the dog" and "I know you're trying to play me off a break".'

Frank's a modern father, he says, and tries to engage with his daughter as much as possible. 'At twenty-five, I was still on the booze. At thirty-five I was running out of puff, and I had patience. That makes a big difference,' he says. Now forty-seven, he's learnt, he says, from the mistakes of his own parents also. He wants his daughter to become strong and independent, with an understanding of her responsibilities. He knows he needs to be present. He's even planned for her to do a self-defence course. Frank wants to arm his daughter with what she needs to make her own way in the world. But it is the difference in his and his wife's approach, and how they communicate, that is presenting a challenge. His wife's immediate defence of his daughter can prevent their child from accepting her responsibilities, and mutes his efforts to be consistent. 'You don't get the choice later in life to have your mum do it, so you've got to learn now,' he says. Frank gives the example of hearing his wife ask their daughter to do something. Their daughter argues. 'I say, "Your mum asked you to do it, now do it."' He is supporting his wife, he believes, being consistent, expecting his daughter to accept her responsibilities. 'But then her mum jumps in to her defence!' And he is sidelined.

Knowing the disparate ways in which males and females communicate is fundamental to parenting, because men and women often see the world through very different lenses. How much they talk or are willing to discuss can vary widely, too. This hit home for me, personally, many years ago when my husband took our twelve-month-old daughter out to lunch with his best mate. As I arrived at the restaurant to pick her up, I looked in through the front window and saw our child in a baby seat, playing with the food she liked and throwing what she didn't on the floor. My husband and his friend seemed oblivious to the mess. Furthermore, they weren't talking to each other either, just eating, in silence. 'Did you see Maddie throwing her food all over the place?' I asked later. 'No,' my husband responded. 'She seemed to be having fun.' 'And why weren't you talking to Jamie?' I asked. 'We were when we had something to say, but you don't have to fill every silence.'

Because men and women connect in such particular ways, how parents work together to convey messages to their children is critical. They need to be in sync. That topic could make a whole book but what does this mean for a girl communicating with her father? Does the way he *respond* make her less amenable to conversation? Or is there just an age where she will be more taciturn, or more comfortable confiding in her mother? That might even suit some fathers. But what about those who want to continue those conversations they shared with their prepubescent daughter? And what role do mothers play here?

The communication divide between fathers and daughters is undeniable, and the thumbnail sketch to how this looks is this: girls who have always been close to their fathers find talking to them easier than their peers; those with similar views to their fathers, especially on politics and current affairs, are more inclined to open up to him; personal stuff is largely directed towards their mothers; and in the search for black and white or a clinical assessment of an issue, girls often seek out their father, who they believe is more likely to provide them with unbiased options. The reasons why girls will limit communications with their father range from their divergent views, a lack of time (particularly on their father's side), and a fear over how their fathers might react.

None of this is a recent dilemma. More than twenty-five years ago, John Gray's *Men are from Mars, Women are from Venus* gave popular understanding to what was happening in homes around the world, selling millions of copies and making its author a wealthy man. More than a quarter of a century later, John Gray sees the same stark difference between the sexes that prompted him to put pen to paper. 'When your daughter first walks, and her mother is at her job, she feels as though she's really missed out,' he says. 'The father hears through his wife. He doesn't feel as though he's missed out as much because he's heard through his wife.'

Men very often connect to their children through their partners. Traditionally, men have taken on the role of breadwinners; their partners fill them in on their newborn's progress when they arrive home from work each evening. This continues as each child grows up. When a child is away on school camp and phones home, her father might answer first. He will often then hand the phone to his partner, because she knows what to say and will have more questions. He feels as though he's connected with the child, says John Gray. 'He can listen on the phone from a distance and hear what his wife says.' Similarly, men and women approach problem-solving in distinct ways. Women talk it out, where men might act it out (they see a problem and want to fix it). Women will often attempt to prevent the problem from developing in the first place. Has my daughter got enough friends? How will she go in this subject? The male and female approaches are both useful. 'Both are important messages for a child to hear,' John Gray says. 'You have to learn in life how to avoid problems but you also have to learn how to deal with problems.'

Certainly, girls say they will opt to seek their fathers out when a problem is overwhelming them and they need options. They say he will offer a rational, almost unemotional view. He won't network the problem with friends; it will be confidential. Girls don't see this as their fathers 'fixing' their problems but rather him providing them with choices. Each of these responses demonstrates why girls seek their fathers out to talk.

> 'If it's a school problem I'll tell Dad because he won't tell the other dads. It's safe with him. Mum will talk to other mums and ask what would happen if this happened to your kid.'

> 'He has sat there with me every night in my first year of high school and it paid off, as I went from failing or only just passing every class to getting the higher end of the grades.'

> 'Mum overthinks things too much, she says this might happen, then this might happen and then this might happen. Geez, it's like she's read horror stories all night.'

> 'He has a really sensible logic so he is always calm.'

> 'If I got a C in Maths, Dad would ask whether I needed a tutor. Mum would just be upset.'

As girls climb into their teens, their privacy is paramount. Sometimes they see their mother as wanting to pry, or wanting to know minutiae they don't want to share.

> 'Mum will work through it too much and go into everything, Dad will just say, "Okay, those kids are

banned from the house; no-one treats my girl like that.
Delete them from social media. Find new friends."'

It is her father's clinical, straight-talking and practical approach, and his lack of judgement, that she is seeking.

'Dad won't sugar-coat something. I like that.'

'Dad says it straight. I like that. Mum doesn't.'

'Dad is less judgemental. I normally go to Mum, but she exaggerates the problem usually. So I end up talking to Dad.'

'Mum dramatises it, so I go to Dad.'

'Yeah. He's kind of like a therapist.'

'He gives me great tips on how to handle situations.'

'I know he will never judge me and will always give me advice from an outside point of view.'

'He is calm.'

'My dad understands that I am not good at everything and I have my strengths and weaknesses.'

'I can talk to Dad about the big things. Like, we had someone pass away and it was Dad who came and got me and told me, not Mum.'

Note that these preferences apply when girls feel in a muddle, or when something is prodigious. On a day-to-day basis, Mum is generally the first port of call. She's easier to chat to and she understands and empathises with many of the issues her daughter might confront, because she's been there before. Personal issues are out of bounds for Dad.

'I go to Dad for schoolwork and Mum for period pain.'

'I do like talking to my dad about school and after-school-related stuff, but not really the emotional stuff.'

'I go to Mum about everyday stuff but Dad about politics and what's happening.'

'Things that are not personal to me, like schoolwork or general topics, are okay. If they are directly about me, then no.'

'I find it easy to talk to my father about philosophical questions but not about girl stuff. I expect that that would be quite normal, though.'

'I find it easy to talk to him about worldly subjects but not so much personal issues.'

Indeed, almost two-thirds of girls say they would go to their mother to talk first. The rest would go to their father, or someone else, including grandparents, a sibling, a friend, teacher or sporting coach. Problems requiring difficult solutions, Maths homework, sports and current affairs topped the issues where fathers would be sought out – ironically reinforcing some of those traditional beliefs our daughters are urged to eschew! As a mother, I found this response, from mid-teens, troubling. Why would our strong, independent girls, who believe in equality and who dislike being treated differently from their brothers, so quickly nominate their father as being the best source for information, schoolwork and sport? While some girls said they would go to their mother first on these issues, it was very common for girls to nominate their father as the first port of call here. But why? It's just a fact, one said, explaining that her mother would hate to be asked about Maths homework. Her friends agreed; one surmising that they were all topics that could be talked about dispassionately. When fathers were asked the same question – whether their daughters would go to them or their partner to talk through an issue – their responses suggested that they were unaware of how often their daughters talked to someone outside the home. They almost always believed their daughters would choose their partner or themselves.

So why aren't daughters drawn to talking with their fathers about the daily stuff – like friendship woes, troubles with a teacher, the unfairness of a situation, issues relating to puberty? What is stopping them?

> *'He thinks I still have the mindset of a nine-year-old, and I can't talk about "growing-up issues" or anything mildly explicit, or politics or anything like that, because I'm "too young to understand".'*

> *'I feel like by opening up to him a bit more our relationship would be able to grow. Though I find it awkward talking to him about deep things like emotions and feelings.'*

> *'I find it really difficult to talk to him about emotional stuff, I think because ever since I was young my dad kind of associated being emotional with being weak, and I just can't shake myself of that mindset.'*

Now in a perfect parenting partnership, conversation with a teen girl might be covered. Parents, on the same page, might work hard, and together, to ensure all bases are covered – even if the consequence is that fathers miss out on those personal chats. But that is to gloss over two issues that were raised repeatedly: first, girls' perceptions that their fathers were unable to communicate the way their mothers could; and secondly, that their fathers were less crucial in their teenage life than they had been in previous years.

'He is not good at communicating.'

'When I was younger I was very much his "princess", as I was very girly compared to the rest of my family. We were quite close. But as I grow older we are quite divided, as he doesn't really know how to talk with me.'

'Most of the time I don't feel like I'm being met halfway so don't put in the effort.'

'I go and try to talk to him but his answers are quite short and he returns to playing games or working on a project. I try watching movies with him and that sort of works . . . at times.'

'When I ring him (from boarding school) I always ask for Mum, and then Dad will get sad and tell Mum he wished I asked for him first, so next time I do, but then he doesn't really have anything to say. I talk to him definitely more at home than Mum.'

Paul Dillon of Drug and Alcohol Research and Training Australia has a strong investment in the wellbeing of young people. He says teens are excellent at exploiting differences in how their parents communicate. 'They are very, very clever at siloing parents off and separating them,' he says. 'They know who the weakest link is. They do this very, very early in their life.' Dillon says some research suggests that children know from as early as the age of three that forum shopping between parents will work in their favour. 'If they know their dad is the weakest link and they can pull the "precocious little daughter" routine, then they will use it.' Put that to a group of girls and embarrassed fidgeting can't hide the fact that there is not a single voice of dissension.

'A common refrain from Dad is: "Go and ask your mother." My dad does that when it comes to sleepovers and stuff. I always ask him first because Mum will say no [and then she will stage a negotiation].'

'I rang Mum up and asked could I buy these new boots. She said "no". I rang Dad and he said "yes" and he just paid for them on his credit card. She doesn't know yet that I've got them.'

'If it is related to my boyfriend, Mum will say "yes" and Dad will say "no". So I would always go to Mum.'

'I just expect Mum to say "no", so I go to Dad . . .'

Paul Dillon says girls are also capable of working out the most likely scenario under which a parent will grant them their wish. He says surveys have shown the best chance of a girl being given what she wants is by asking her mother while she (her mother) is on the phone. It boosts her chances further if her mother is chatting to a good friend. But they'll use the best ammunition at their disposal to get the right answer from Dad, too. 'If I want to get out of school,' says one girl, 'I say I'm not feeling well. It's hard because he's a doctor so he knows when I'm faking it. But if I just tell him I've got period cramps, he's just out of there.' This example was not isolated. Sue says she opens the conversation with her father with the fact that she has period pain. She then asks for what she wants. 'He says, "I don't want to hear about your womanly issues,"' and grants her her wish.

But mothers usually get to have the final say.

'The other day I wanted to go to a party. I asked Dad first and he said yes, but just check with your mum. And then Mum gets the final say.'

'Dad will offer advice but Mum has the final say.'

The remarkable element about the issue of girls talking to their fathers was the consistency of answers, irrespective of whether the girls were aged eleven or seventeen. Perhaps one difference was that at the younger end, girls struggled to understand why they found it easier to talk to their mothers. 'Why is it easier to talk to Mum than Dad?' one twelve-year-old asked. This also from a twelve-year-old: 'I wish he could spend time with me and just ask me whether I'm alright.' This girl believed her father would wait until her mother told him that she was struggling with an issue and that he should become involved. Another said: 'Dad would say friendships are Mum's department.'

Mothers know they hold the key to communication with their daughters. Almost unanimously, they believe their daughters would first bring a personal or emotional matter to them over their male partners. Here are some testimonies from them:

'When she got her period I was away for work for a few days and she texted me. She never – and still nearly two years later hasn't – let on to him. He helps her when she has trouble with homework or school assignments. She'll rarely come to me for a problem in that area.'

'The relationship with her dad is fun, full of banter and kind-hearted teasing. She would definitely see me as being more understanding of problems she faces. Her dad is one of three brothers, so he sometimes doesn't understand the delicacy of teenage-girl emotions.'

'I think she likes to keep her relationships with her dad as uncomplicated and as fun as possible. I am left to pick up the rest!'

Associate Professor Dr Michael Nagel from Queensland's University of the Sunshine Coast colours in this picture. An expert in educational psychology and child development, and the father of a daughter, he still finds himself bemused by the mysteries thrown up by the different ways women and men see things. 'One of the biggest differences between males and females of all ages – and you see this early in life but it becomes more pronounced in adolescence and adulthood – is that females are very good at processing emotional stimuli in social contexts,' he says. 'We know that most women are very good at processing emotional stimuli and men are not really good at it. We tend not to see the emotions, we tend to mistake them, we tend not to read them very well and for all intents and purposes we tend to avoid that if we can.' This is not code for men copping out; it shows that it is a difficult thing for men to do – a point also made clear by Professor Ruben Gur from the Perelman School of Medicine at the University of Pennsylvania, USA. Professor Gur and his colleagues took male and female volunteers aged nineteen to forty and scanned their brains while they were undertaking a task: observing images of a face and nominating whether the displayed emotion was happy or sad. Researchers found that women were faster and more accurate than men in determining the emotion displayed in the image. And their brains looked different too. By and large, only a small part of women's brains lit up during the test, signifying that they didn't think the task was particularly difficult. For men, all areas of the brain lit up like a house on fire – red, yellow and orange! Professor Nagel says other studies have followed this example. 'Across the board, women were far better at reading emotions – simple emotions of whether you are happy or not happy – with greater expediency, greater efficiency and with less effort. Men really struggled,' he says.

The relevance to fathers communicating with their daughters is this: men are not good at reading emotional cues in real time, so the default position, for many men, is to avoid it as much as possible. Professor Nagel says that means it is easier for fathers to say 'ask Mum' or 'let me fix it for you'. Fathers were less likely to want to traverse emotions ranging from happy, sad, angry, frustrated, ad infinitum. 'It's just, "This is what we should do and everything will be great".' And that is precisely what fathers might typically do. Men will be more comfortable knowing the details required to address a situation. They won't need, or want, to consider the personalities involved, or the feelings and emotions, and the whys and wherefores around it. 'For a lot of males that's just not something we're comfortable with doing and we really don't do it well,' Professor Nagel says.

Educators see the same difference in approach when a parent sits across the office desk, trying to sort out a difficulty with his or her child. Usually it is the student's mother who attends the meeting. The meeting may be prompted by a friendship issue, or debate over a discipline handed out to her daughter. The mother might even be advocating on behalf of her daughter, or demanding she be given special consideration for something. 'Rarely are dads there for that,' a private school principal says. A public school principal concurs: 'I hardly ever see fathers come to one-on-one meetings.' A third says this: 'If I walk into the office and see a mother waiting to see me, or more than one, I know it's a normal day. If a dad's there, it escalates everything. I could be a few hours away from being sued!' He says that half jokingly, but his point is this: mothers and fathers of daughters communicate with each other, their daughters and the school very differently. Fathers might be calmer, less judgemental, less inclined to discuss issues, but they are more inclined to act decisively. Mothers might be more emotionally involved with their daughters than they should be sometimes, quick to jump to their defence, able to talk on a much deeper level and provide knowledge born of experience.

The problem is when those different approaches don't work together. That's when a girl is likely to find herself slipping through the cracks. 'My wife has to explain what's going on to me sometimes,' says Andrew, the father of four girls. He says there are many topics, especially relating to friendships, that he struggles to grasp. 'I'm intrigued, because it seems so different between boys and girls, especially with friendships,' he says. His daughters might have a friendship dilemma and the re-telling is full of 'she said' and then 'So-and-so said' and then 'someone else said'. 'It's unbelievable! My wife said it can be typical of girls – but they get so emotional about it!' He says he and his wife work hard to present a strong parenting platform. In their house, it came down to good communication between parents, and each valuing the other's role. That includes avoiding the problem at the heart of Frank's story: how he and his wife communicated differently. Differences of opinion between parents are best worked out between parents, without their daughter/s being involved. It's sometimes harder than it sounds. One principal tells the story of receiving two emails from parents of the same girl – a delightful student who had not been placed in the same class as her usual group of friends. Her father sent an email saying how important it was for teen girls to stand on their own two feet. Some of them, in his words, even needed to 'toughen up'. He applauded the decision. A few days later the girl's mother also dropped a note to the principal. She hoped the school understood that her daughter was feeling 'a bit sad'. Being placed in a class without any friends was a big step for her.

Same family, same daughter, and a completely different message!

7

Connecting

One night not long ago, at a hall in central Victoria, a teen girl arrived at a father–daughter night with a live yabby. It was in a little takeaway food tub, filled with water and decorated with greenery. The girls and fathers had been asked to bring along a 'treasure' – something important to them that reflected on their relationship with each other. The organisers asked her about the significance of the yabby. 'This is what I do with my dad,' she said. 'This is what I love.'

Bill Jennings runs one of the many programs schools host to focus on the relationships between parents and children. Different schools adopt different programs: some are based around mother and son; many are also focused on mother and daughter. On this night it was Jennings' Time & Space program for fathers and daughters being played out in a small country hall. 'That was the first living treasure we'd had brought to one of the nights,' he says. Fathers usually brought along a photograph of their child as a newborn, with Dad wearing a grin that stretched from one ear to the other. Others brought the first card they'd received from their daughters (who had no idea it had been stashed away for almost a decade in a bottom drawer). Shoes, too, were popular – ballet shoes, a girl's first runners, a tiny pair of dress shoes that her father couldn't part with but had never revealed he'd kept. The girls often opted for something signalling an activity they shared with their father, like the yabby. 'One of the things that dads are good at with their daughters is being the person who does the doing things – together,' Jennings says. Going to the football, watching the swimming on television, playing beachside cricket, mucking around in the pool, hiking, camping, running, learning to drive, making a kite, planning a school project, bike riding, learning to fish, watching a movie at the local cinemas . . . activities. Ask a girl about a searing memory showing a bond with their father, and chances are it will involve an activity. The Time & Space program aims to give girls a perspective on what it is like to walk in their parents' shoes, and an insight for parents on being a teen in a world packed with social media, peer assessment and wall-to-wall marketing. Jennings' father–daughter program is only one of those successfully used by schools, and it centres on three conversations. First, fathers will talk to a teen, but not their daughter, and the two will ask questions. These might relate to how they think the night will unfold, or what they both think is important in a relationship between a teen girl and a male role model. Secondly, girls chat with a peer, and fathers chat with another father. This gives fathers an opportunity they might rarely take up: the chance to use a peer sounding board. Then, after interacting with a panel of girls and dads who have previously undertaken the program, the girls sit with the male who accompanied them, most often their father or carer. That's when they share a 'treasure'; a memento that they've chosen to present to each other.

Seeking the views of about 1300 girls for this book taught me so much, and strong themes developed that became the foundation for this project. The one that stood out was the similarity in responses from those girls who shared a robust relationship with their father. Three answers turned up, over and over again; the bond that working the land created; the signficance of shared beliefs; and the connection between sport and a good father–daughter relationship.

First, girls who were raised in the country and wanted to work on the land boasted a treasured relationship with their fathers. Many of those girls were at boarding school, and while they would talk to their mothers often, they really missed their fathers. Adelaide principal Kevin Tutt says: 'The engagement of dads in boarding life is really obvious. Dads will really make the effort to be here for their girls and not just in sport but across the board as much as they can,' he says. Dr Linda Evans, from Toowoomba's Fairholme College, sees the same bond forged by fathers and daughters, in rural areas. 'Typically, most of our boarders are from working properties. Most of our boarders will go home and work over the holidays and invariably that's more likely to be with Dad than it is with Mum,' she says.

A second theme that surfaced during interviews with the girls – and backed by experts – related to a father's opinions or beliefs. Girls who shared the same views as their fathers, particularly at around the ages of sixteen and seventeen, developed a solid alliance, and they attributed the connection to that. The converse was true, too: those who disagreed strongly with their father's opinions believed a significant gap existed in their relationship.

The third was that girls who played a sport their father loved and was actively involved in (whether coaching, ferrying them to and from training, or watching them) enjoyed a lovely bond with their fathers. It didn't only have to be an organised school or club sport. Girls who regularly ran or went bike riding or camping with their fathers enjoyed a similarly good relationship. This response was so strong that I went home and jotted down a long list of activities my girls could do with their father, my husband. The power of the connection engendered through sport was reinforced by educators, teen counsellors and researchers.

Warm father–daughter relationships don't require these three themes to succeed, but they certainly highlight how that connection can be built. Music might offer another means of connection, particularly with the revival of some of those bands that have lengthened the generation between father and daughter (like AC/DC, Frankie Valli and Meatloaf).

It's not unusual to see fathers moved to tears at Time & Space events. 'There's a lot of tenderness in the evening,' Bill Jennings says. 'I think the reason they take it up is because families are really busy, and they actually get given an opportunity to have a conversation that they thought they might like to have but never get the chance to do.' Mothers and daughters share a special relationship, but fathers should never discount the influence they have on their daughters, he says.

Polly Flanagan, principal of Shelford Girls' Grammar in Victoria says the value of this program showed in the feedback that flowed in after it:

'I found this experience very good for me because I now realise how very little time I spend with him.'

'It was a great opportunity to talk and learn new things about your dad.'

'We haven't really talked about these things before, so I liked being able to talk.'

'This might be one of the most memorable nights of my childhood.'

'I learnt so much about a father's perspective, and now I know what it is like.'

And this from a father who attended:

'As open as my daughter has been for eighteen months.'

Schools have become active in creating events around fathers and daughters – like breakfasts, dances and Father's Day lunches – for two reasons. First, many mirror events already operating for mothers and daughters; and secondly, there's compelling evidence that girls can benefit from a warm connection with their fathers.

'I'd love Dad to get on a horse with me. He's always there. He'll help us saddle up and do everything and once we get on, he says, "That's it." I'd love him to come riding with me.'

'Dad and I love rugby and cricket. Mum's not really interested in that.'

'I can talk to him when we are driving to sport. Sometimes it takes ages and we just talk and talk.'

On occasions, girls said they took up a sport with the specific purpose of making their father proud, or as an attempt to bond with him. 'My dad was really, really good at water polo and also Aussie Rules. So this year I did Aussie Rules and I started water polo. We bond over it now, but I really want to do well – for him,' Manny, fifteen, says.

Research by Baylor University has shown that a 'turning point' in a father–daughter relationship can be the activity they share, beating other significant events like a daughter marrying, leaving home or having her own children. The study involved forty-three daughters and an equal number of unrelated fathers. Participants were asked to nominate the moment their own father–daughter relationship changed – irrespective of what that change was. Shared activities topped the list for both the daughters and the fathers, with researchers finding the activity that brought them closer was a sporting activity. 'Sports were the biggest deal that brought us together. Playing sports created a huge bond between my dad [and me], and that connected us a lot,' one girl told researchers. 'I used to love it when my dad would take off work to come coach my softball team,' another said. 'As sports became a bigger and bigger part of my life, my father and I got closer and closer,' a third said. The most common answer, when fathers were asked, mirrored that of the girls. 'We didn't spend much time together until she started playing sports,' one said. 'Sports gave us a bond that she did not have with her mother or siblings. It was our time to be together,' another said. The study showed researchers that 'sport not only gave fathers and daughters something in common, but provided them with something to talk about as well, which apparently opened the lines of communication on the subjects.'[1]

Professor Philip Morgan from the University of Newcastle's School of Education is the architect of the DADEE (Dads and Daughters Exercising and Empowered) program. It engages fathers and daughters specifically through sport, and is believed to be the first of its kind in the world. Through the program, girls' fitness and resilience is built through rough-and-tumble play, as well as other activities and fathers' knowledge is boosted through evidence-based parenting strategies. Professor Morgan says that fathers frequently didn't think that their girls were interested in sport and physical activity, despite their belief that it offered physiological, emotional and psychological advantages. The program, run over several weeks and aimed at primary school aged girls, turns stereotypes – like 'pink is for girls and blue is for boys' – on their head, and improves girls' sporting skills as well as building their self-confidence and resilience.

Professor Morgan says the physical confidence was due, in part, to a new awareness of gender bias and a refusal to buy into traditional stereotypes. Fathers, key motivators in girls' lives, could play a crucial role in doing that.

You'll get no argument there from Australian Rugby Sevens coach Tim Walsh, who also coached the women's team to a world series championship, an Olympic gold medal and Commonwealth Games silver medal. He says there was 100 per cent tie-in between a girl, her engagement with her father or father-figure, and her ability to perform well in a contact sport like rugby. 'I speak to the players – nearly every single one of them has two or three brothers, and all of the coaches have sisters or daughters. One of the biggest influences in their lives is their family, and their fathers,' he says. Walsh took on the job of coaching the women's team when he was playing in Italy many years ago, and the power of the girls' fathers soon became obvious. 'When a dad said something it resonated a lot more; it had a lot more power behind it,' he says. He says that that was so obvious he put his mind to a 'father's club', where he and the dads could together nut out how to reshape and deal with the tricky lead-up to big competitions. 'The tighter that father–daughter relationship is, the more confident they are, the more emotionally aware they are,' he says. He says he believes, after being involved with men's and women's sport, that there is a significant difference in how the different genders approach competitive sport: girls have to be happy to win; boys have to win to be happy. 'When the girls were nervous and under pressure, it didn't work,' he says. The happier they were – as a group – the more confident they felt and the better they performed. The role of their fathers was critical in generating this happiness. Whereas mothers could worry about the contact nature of the sport, fathers were supportive – but never pushy. 'The dads were in that space where they could empathise and talk to the girls a lot more and be very proud of them too,' Walsh says. Robyn Kronenberg, a former school principal and education consultant at Bond University, says sport provided fathers with a unique opportunity to engage with their daughters. 'With time there has been an increase in fathers being conscious of the relationship with their children, where in the past it was the father–son thing,' she says. The big increase in father–daughter engagement has come, specifically, around sport.

Other programs aimed at connecting fathers and daughters don't always focus on sport, but *activity* is a central focus on many. Rite Journey, a program conducted in various forms, including a year-long one for girls, has been used by St Margaret's College in Christchurch, New Zealand. Gillian Simpson, the school's former executive principal, says part of that program requires girls and their fathers to complete a project together. As part of that, girls have to learn all sorts of skills – from driving tractors, to fishing, building and baking. 'The girls say that the program is one of the highlights of the year ... and there are often some quite teary dads at the end, when the girls do their presentation,' she says.

Fathers and daughters don't necessarily have to undertake organised programs to make connections. Psychologist and author Andrew Fuller took his Year 9 daughter to Sri Lanka to help at an elephant orphanage, as a father–daughter social-action activity. Back home, he also would sometimes wake his children up and grant them the day off school, to go on a 'magical mystery tour'. 'I would take them and show them something that was just interesting,' he says. It started when the eldest was eight, and continued through their teenage years. 'If you don't have shared experiences, it's hard to have shared conversations,' he says. He also urges fathers to seek out their daughters' opinions about particular issues so that there is a very clear message that he values her intellect rather than her image or her appearance or her compliance.

Tamworth principal David Smith says being a parent of daughters has been his hardest undertaking. 'But it's also the best thing that I've ever done,' he says. As a principal, he sees the same fields of interest as already identified – that is, sport, a connection built around farming or rural life, and similar views – as being the things that connect fathers and daughters. He offers another connector, too, saying he believes that those fathers who showed their daughter affection developed and maintained an easy bond. 'Girls often learn about affection from significant males in their lives, and Dad is the biggest one of those,' he says. 'I think the attitude of the dad and the behaviour of the dad around affection and self-confidence is a really vital thing,' he says.

Clinical psychologist Kirrilie Smout, who is the director of Developing Minds Psychology and Education, wants dads to coach their teen girls. 'We know that the girls have skill gaps. There are things that they can't do well yet – and they don't know that they can't do them well because they're teenagers, and sometimes teenagers don't know what they don't know.' Smout gives examples like sticking to tasks, and organisation, and even managing conflict. 'What dads can do is think, "How do I coach my daughter in this?" We want them to get alongside their teenage girls and be really actively coaching them.'

Sport. Doing activities together. Growing up on a farm. Shared outlooks or opinions. A shared love of music. Displaying affection. Working on a social activity together. Coaching them. All are connectors that can grow the bond between fathers and daughters. Dr Briony Scott from Wenona is one of a dozen experts who recommend a regular father–daughter 'date', like breakfast every second Friday. 'You build the relationship as part of the ritual, and when life gets tough, as it invariably will, and they start to withdraw, you say, "Well, every second Friday,

we are having breakfast." You keep the connection open.'
It doesn't have to revolve around deep conversation; the
crucial element is the shared, independent relationship.
'And that independent relationship is pure gold. If there's
not a dad around, an uncle is just fine. A grandfather is
just fine . . . as long as there is a male influence, or a male
role model around,' she says.

Liza Coutts is director of communications at what is
often touted as Britain's top girls' school, St Paul's Girls'
School. She is also the co-founder of Dads4Daughters,
a program that challenges sexism in the workplace and
which has now spread to America and Africa. She says
fathers could move mountains when they advocated for
their daughters, and their daughters dreamed big. Bringing
that together could transform workplace culture. 'In the
past, a father thought it was his role to take his daughter
down the aisle. That analogy has now gone and this is
the equivalent of the father leading his daughter into a
really great workplace.' Dads4Daughters began a couple
of years ago after a survey of alumni found more than 70
per cent had witnessed or encountered gender inequality in
the workplace and the vast majority believed men should
do more to achieve a cultural change. St Paul's, the UK
Girls' Schools Association and fifty other girls' schools,
along with big companies including UBS and Ernst &
Young, are now involved in the program where fathers
with daughters at school pledge to try and change the

culture where they work. Fathers – who include some of the country's top financiers – are challenged to take an 'unconscious bias' test. Vivienne Durham, chief executive of the UK Girls' Schools Association, says systemic change followed fathers thinking about their own daughters' experiences. 'Would you like your daughter to work in the culture you've got? Would you like your daughter to be a member of this board? Are the working habits, the working hours and the working practices of this organisation what you would like your daughter to experience when she goes into the world of work? When you make it that personal, that makes it quite powerful.'

So how do you gauge if it is working? Liza Coutts relays the story of a senior national banker who was recently asked to sit on a panel. He found out the panel was to be made up of three other men, and declined. 'He said to me that was with his Dads4Daughters' hat on,' she says.

8

What dads can offer

It is one comment from one sixteen-year-old, but it sums up what girls said over and over again. 'I feel like my dad is disappointed in me less often than my mum is,' Heidi says. 'Mum will get disappointed in me over little things like not emptying the dishwasher. If Dad is disappointed in me, it's over something bigger and it seems more important.' Taylor is also sixteen: 'If my dad is disappointed in me, that would be really different to me than if it was my mum. It would affect me differently.' Jenni says the same. 'If I'm in trouble with Dad I'm terrified, because it doesn't happen often. When he speaks, I know it is big. So if he says something I tend to listen more.'

That ability to 'not sweat the small stuff' and pick the issues is, if executed well, something that can gift fathers the ear of their daughters. It is something substantial and concrete that fathers can offer, at home, but it's only one of a host of qualities that girls nominate as being important to their wellbeing.

'Dad gets straight to the point, so I understand what he says. It's a straight-up answer.'

'Mum inflates things. The arguments are more subdued when Dad's involved.'

'If he doesn't think something is good for you, he suggests another path.'

'Sometimes Mum cries about my mark. It's my mark, not hers! That just makes me feel worse. Dad says it's okay if I tried my best.'

'He wants me to choose a path that will make me happy. He has a firm belief that if I make the decision that will make me happy, security and success will follow. My mum is the one who puts more pressure on my academic performance.'

'His wish is for me to become a doctor and attend a good university. However, above all he wants me to be happy and live a happy life. He hopes that I have my own family and visit him often when I'm older.'

'He wants me to not go to uni and either do a trade or go to the mines like him. I think he also wants me to not be complicated and be really easygoing.'

A calm port in a storm, picking the pivotal issues, being direct and using specific language, being rational, offering alternatives, accepting his daughter for who she is, being real: these are attributes that girls praised in their fathers. They are also the qualities that can benefit daughters as they journey through adolescence. This isn't to say that mothers don't offer these qualities, and many more, but fathers who struggle with communication, and a teenage girl who is drawn to her mother, should not underestimate what he has to offer his daughter. The importance of providing time, of listening, of being present in her life, of granting her the security to develop views and prosecute them, and of role-modelling respectful relationships are all explored elsewhere. But what else can a 21st-century father offer his daughter to provide her a strong, stable and positive jumping-off place into adulthood?

What stood out repeatedly in the girls' answers was how they welcomed what their father wanted for them. A small group of fathers was pushy, demanding their daughters achieve beyond what she thought she could. 'He won't be satisfied unless I get into medicine,' one said. 'My dad wants me to work hard in school and become a doctor, preferably a brain surgeon,' another said. Others said their fathers wanted them to gain entry into Law and Medicine, and girls whose parents lived overseas said that often. School counsellors report that, too: fathers who apply so much pressure to perform academically that their daughters sit frozen in exam rooms. But most girls believe their fathers' expectations are both positive and comforting. This differs from what they think of their mothers' expectations of them. Girls believe their mums want them to achieve at higher levels than is possible. School leaders, too, say while fathers could be 'volcanic', in the words of one, and demand their daughters achieve 'unattainable results', they were less set on that than mothers, who had a clear idea of the path they wanted their daughters to take. 'We've got a couple of dads who are very hard on their daughters, but generally speaking I think it's true that right at the coalface it is women, and that is because more of them work part-time and so they're more present in the schools,' one principal said.

So what do girls see as their father's expectations of them? Topping the list, by a strong margin, is their belief that their fathers want them to be happy. Working hard and doing their best came in second, and staying safe was third. This was reflected across the board – in single-gender schools, in co-educational schools, at boarding schools and in day schools, in city areas and rural areas, across the country.

'Of course my dad wants me to be successful in life, but he also wants me to be happy. I think he would prefer it if I went to university, and as for my future profession he really just wants me to be happy with what I am doing.'

'He doesn't have expectations of me, he just wants the best for me and for me to be happy.'

'He's happy as long as I'm trying my best.'

'University, probably working interstate or overseas, but he wants me to be happy and safe more than anything else.'

'Although he wants me to be happy he also would want me to be successful and have a good job, but he wouldn't pressure me to do anything that I don't want to.'

'I reckon he just wants me to be happy and be optimistic to face the world around me. But I'm sure he does not want me to be a police officer or in some dangerous job.'

'He wants me to go to university, travel and basically live every day like it could be your last.'

'I think he expects and would like me to go to university (and become a doctor), but I know that he would respect whatever I would like to do.'

'My dad doesn't really have any expectations for work, but he has always wanted me to have a certain level of respect for myself and the people around me.'

'My dad talked to me about this. He wants me to be happy and to do my best in school and with everything I do.'

Girls articulate how welcome their fathers' expectations are; a 'relief' to many of them who are trying to juggle so many balls. They appreciate that their fathers are not trying to make them into someone they are not, and that they value their happiness and safety over career choice. Parenting expert Maggie Dent says many fathers see that if 'my daughter is happy, I've done my job', whereas women often put constant expectations on their daughters (as well as themselves). 'The thing I know that guts dads most is to see their daughters particularly, but any of their children, struggling and being sad, because it triggers that sense of "I haven't done my job, I feel powerless to fix this",' she says. The rider on all this, though, as the girls point out, is an expectation by their fathers that they try their best. If they did that, life would unfold as it should.

When a group of girls was questioned about this, they largely stated that they did not believe this meant their father lacked ambition for them career-wise, or that he believed their potential in the workforce was limited. An irony jumps out here, because as you will read later, many girls believe their fathers treat their brothers very differently from the way they treat them. The girls nevertheless believe their fathers want them to aim high, and try, and succeed – but that their happiness is paramount. 'I know that he just wants me to be the best version of myself I can be,' says one girl. 'If he has any other expectations, he doesn't tell me.'

Ask principals, school nurses, parenting experts and school counsellors what a father can offer his daughter, and it comes down to many of the issues we've discussed. But one comment encapsulates it: 'It's role-modelling.' Robyn Kronenberg says, 'Daughters need to see both what their mother can do as a person, not only as a mother, but they also need to see their father as a person. They need to see what good citizenship is from good people – male and female.' Gillian Simpson says a healthy father–daughter relationship is a strong marker for an adolescent girl. 'It's for girls to see how a good man is in life. A good man is a role model; a good father, but also a good person – a person who serves and cares for others.' If a teenage girl can have confidence knowing how a man ought to act, she will be more 'positive in any working environment with men, or in a marriage or in relationships', she says. Certainly it helps from the moment boys appear on the scene, because it allows girls to set boundaries, expect respect and look for those attributes they see in their father. 'It gives them the right expectations about a relationship and how they should be treated,' Simpson says. When experts are asked what a father can offer his daughter, this comes up repeatedly: the influence he has on his daughter's relationship, with other males, as she matures. Girls are also constantly looking for cues, and pick up on how their father treats their mother. Some experts label that as the 'greatest thing a father can offer his daughter'. A father is the primary male figure in a girl's life, and is the cornerstone of how she develops bonds with men, her whole life. That role is magnified in those cases where girls do not have a male sibling, or where they attend an all-girls school. Her father might be the only male with whom she shares ongoing constant contact.

What are the characteristics and views of Mum and Dad that girls will want to mirror? What will they eschew? Victorian principal Polly Flanagan says that girls, faced with a rapidly changing world, are being challenged to know what values they hold dear, and a parent's contribution there was paramount – 'otherwise they will bob around like corks,' she warns. Another principal describes it in this way: fathers are 'islands' in a storm, and girls need to know that that is where they can take shelter, and also where they can build themselves into who they want to be. Both principals raised the value of school engagement – for fathers as well as for mothers. Flanagan says parents and schools, working as partners, can hugely benefit teen girls. 'We can't do our job properly in this school unless parents communicate with us, and they can't do their job properly if we don't communicate with them,' she says. Those days where we might have dropped our children at the school gate at age six in the knowledge that they'd graduate at sixteen, skilled and ready to take on the world, are long gone.

Research the world over supports the long list of ways fathers can help grow their fierce daughters into awesome women. Research has indicated that mothers are their daughters' most important role models, but the same research does not dispute that fathers are the 'template' for what girls' future interactions with men might be like. This emphasises the point made earlier about girls seeing their future relationships through the prism of what they have learnt from their father. 'So how much,' Professor Renée Spencer of Boston University asks, 'does their father convey that he respects girls and women? What are the messages that he delivers about what a girl is supposed to be like and what makes her acceptable?'[2] A father can assist in building critical thinking skills which allow a girl to discern fact from fiction, give her the ability to believe in herself, and trust in her own decisions. Fathers who espouse gender equality are also shown, over and over, to raise girls who are ambitious as they grow up. Likewise, a strong relationship with one's father has been found to motivate a girl to excel academically. Author Linda

Nielsen, a professor of educational and adolescent psychology at Wake Forest University, USA, says daughters whose fathers have been engaged and supportive throughout the years of their upbringing are more likely to graduate from college and nab the 'higher paying, more demanding jobs traditionally held by males'. 'This helps explain why girls who have no brothers are overly represented among the world's political leaders: they tend to receive more encouragement from their fathers to be high achievers,' she says.[3] Writer Jackie Bischof, in her article 'Here's what dads can do at home to help their daughters grow into successful leaders', explains how those fathers who have faith in their daughters' ability to confront obstacles – and who verbalise that confidence – may also prepare young girls to defend themselves when confronted with sexist views. 'Pakistani education activist Malala Yousafzai, who won the Nobel Peace Prize in 2014, has always had her father's absolute backing,' she writes. 'He did, after all, name his first-born daughter after a 19th century Pashtun warrior heroine.'[4]

The list of what fathers can confer upon their daughters goes on. They can empower daughters by helping them articulate their arguments, teach them patience by listening, encourage them to take calculated risks, teach them practical skills (like how to use a hammer and nail, change a tyre and set up a tent). 'You need to teach her the same sort of things that are important for your son,' Maggie

Dent says. 'She can be strong. She can be as fit. As she goes into adolescence, your job is to equip her with life skills.' She says if a girl is taught life skills, she will not need a male to do those tasks later on. 'She can choose to have a man but she won't need one to fix those little things, because in the end, that's what they thought their place was – to do it for us. But in today's world we're saying, "help me do it for myself".' Fathers can also teach their daughters the value of saying sorry, open their eyes to a host of careers, particularly in the STEM field, to be brave in the face of fear, and to speak up when they – or someone else – is wronged. Mothers are pivotal in many of these areas too, but it has been shown, repeatedly, that fathers matter in their daughters' wellbeing in a unique way.

What goes around comes around, too, with girls able to help their fathers – and the community at large – understand many of those 'soft skills' now considered instrumental to our future. This shouldn't be undervalued, and has been borne out in delightful American research wherein the decisions of 400 CEOs – mainly men – were studied. Henrik Cronqvist, Professor of Finance at the University of Miami, and Frank Yu, Associate Professor of Finance at the China Europe International Business School, say they found having a daughter has an impact on the way CEOs run their companies, and the effect being magnified if their daughter is the first-born. 'The most significant impact has to do with corporate social responsibility issues related to diversity, which previous research has shown includes everything from whether companies provide childcare and flexitime, to their reluctance to lay off staff, and their penchant for sharing profit with employees. It also covers how women, minorities and/or the disabled are treated,' they say. 'We found that, in general, the groups tend to fare better at firms with CEOs who have daughters.'[5]

Phillip Heath, head of Barker College in Sydney, has led schools – co-educational and single-sex, large and small – since 1995 and he says the role of male teachers here should also be valued. 'It's way more important than we used to imagine,' he says. 'There is not a positive narrative around maleness at present, and the presence of male educators who are intellectually attractive, worthy and of sufficient nobility of character to warrant the title "teacher" is essential for both boys and girls.' This is particularly the case where girls are growing up in homes without a male role model. But worryingly, the number of male teachers is continuing to decline. Dr Vaughan Cruickshank, the father of two daughters aged four and three, says the percentage of male primary school teachers has dropped from about 30 per cent in the '80s down to 18 per cent. That number didn't discriminate, either. Dr Cruickshank, from the University of Tasmania, says the figures included principals and physical education specialists – so the actual number of male teachers in the classroom would be well below 18 per cent. The reasons for this are varied, but Dr Cruickshank nominates a fear of physical contact as a key one. 'They feel that it's quite acceptable for their female teaching colleagues to give an upset child a hug, but they're very unsure if that acceptance extends to them,' he says. Dr Cruickshank says male teachers also face suspicion, sometimes, from others for even choosing education as a profession. 'There can be some quite negative perceptions out there that certainly do seem to play on some men's minds.' His research found that male teachers dealt with the fear and uncertainty around these issues by employing a 'strict no-contact policy for their own self-protection'. This meant the use of humour, playing sports with students at lunchtime, setting up their classrooms to 'minimise incidental physical contact', never being one-on-one with students, and even moving to a public location to talk to students.

This point demands greater exploration. Principals concede it is difficult terrain for men. 'But if we can get this right it will be great for the fathers and the girls,' one principal says. 'At the end of the day, these girls need to understand what their values in life are, why their families think they're important, and they need to see them lived out. And I think many men do that well, but there's a lot of self-doubt at the moment.' This principal says the sexual assault revelations that started with Harvey

Weinstein, and Australia's Royal Commission into the sexual abuse of children, had understandably created an atmosphere of wariness, and she knew some fathers worried about even hugging their daughter in public because they were 'second-guessing whether others [were] wondering about their association'. 'It's a difficult place to be, I think,' she says. These comments were reflected by others, and brought home the value of having more strong male teachers, as a norm, in our schools. 'The girls love them,' one principal says. Another principal says that at her school the male teachers won the students' 'best teacher' category year after year. Last year, at her school, students were invited to dress up as someone they admired. One of her male English teachers discovered he was being followed by a group of girls in peculiar costume. 'Why are they all dressed up as Sherlock Holmes?' he asked her. 'Surely they don't want to be Sherlock Holmes!' They don't, she retorted. 'They are dressed up as you!' She explained to me, 'Our girls need strong female role models and they need strong male role models, and they need to see men and women working well together.'

Dr Cruickshank is not alone in pointing to the worrying trend of declining male educators. Dr Kevin McGrath, a researcher and former primary school teacher, believes male teachers might be extinct in Australian primary schools within fifty years. This is not something that reflects what the community at large – including children – want.

Dr McGrath, a couple of years ago, asked Year 6 boys and girls and their parents if they wanted more male teachers. 'They were saying, overwhelmingly, "yes",' he says. Girls were concerned about going into high school and not knowing how to interact with a male teacher. 'From an education point of view it's about children developing gender knowledge,' Dr McGrath says. 'School settings are places where people learn what is in the curriculum, but they learn a whole lot more than that. They learn what it is to be male and female and where they fit in that continuum and what masculinity is and what femininity is. Where there aren't many male teachers, that knowledge becomes limited to other sources, and sometimes they're not positive sources either.'

The reason why having men in schools is so important is that without it some girls will travel through home and school life without a significant male role model. In addition to that, if the only male staffer at a high school is the principal, it doesn't provide a true reflection of the world; it just perpetuates the view that males dominate. Dr McGrath says that is one of the reasons why more male teachers are needed. 'It breaks up those views of male dominance and gives a more realistic view for children of the world.' Some schools have bucked this trend – for example, Wenona in Sydney has, over time, increased the proportion of male teachers from 5 per cent to 40 per cent, and Seymour College in Adelaide this year is making big inroads too, as others are – but the pool of male teachers as a whole continues to dry up. The absence of male teachers makes what a father at home can grant his daughter all the more important. But the more good examples of adult males in her life, the more male role models she is able to draw on. It broadens a girl's understanding to learn that some men like poetry and others enjoy foreign languages.

Two final points of reflection here: first, some schools said they found it difficult to advocate strongly for more men when women were missing out in many other industries. That is understandable – but surely, as a community, equality in employment should be seen across the board, not just in one sector? The second point relates to that. If role-modelling is crucial to girls' development – that is, that they learn what they see – what message is sent by the fact that it is routine to find a male running an all-girls school, but try to find a female educator running an all-boys school in Australia? Good luck!

A father, as a good role model at home, can have a gigantic influence on his daughter's life. The girls say that; experts parrot that; research backs it up. But what about those girls who do not *have* a good male role model at home?

9

Absent dads

Annie is fifteen. Clever. Articulate. And so far, she's sat back as her peers keenly answer questions. That is, at least, until the topic of 'absent fathers' is raised. 'My father is an anaesthetist,' she says, without a hint of pride. 'I'm in bed every night when he comes home from work, we've got to be quiet on Saturdays because he needs to catch up on sleep, so I really only get to see him on Sundays.' Her relationship, she says, is more cordial than warm. She stops, and you can see she almost feels bad revealing this to everyone sitting around the table, so she quickly explains that she wants for nothing. Family holidays are overseas. She has been skiing, on and off, since she was a tot. She was one of the first in her friendship group to get the new Apple iPhone. But along the way, she feels as though she's missed out too. 'We just don't spend much time together,' she says. Would she spend time with him now, given the chance? 'Probably.' But it would be more difficult. It's almost too late. She's got her own friends. She confides in her mother if she needs help. She's used to working out the things she might have asked her father. She's managed without him, so far, so perhaps she doesn't need him anymore? Annie isn't alone, and her story is repeated in other interviews. The plot's the same, but their fathers' jobs change – from lawyers to farmers, small business owners to tradesmen. Living under the same roof, they rarely sit and talk one-on-one with their father. When asked how long ago it was that they talked to their dads for a ten-minute stretch, these were some of their answers:

'I don't think I ever have.'

'Hardly ever.'

'Like never. We never really talk one-on-one and we don't do family discussions. If we talk as a whole family it mostly ends in an argument.'

'I haven't sat down and talked with my father for ten minutes for years.'

That doesn't mean they wouldn't, if the opportunity presented itself.

'Sometimes I wish I could talk to him for at least ten minutes or more, but he always seems busy.'

Dad's work schedule was usually the impediment to a more-than-fleeting chat.

'Once a month, because Dad is very busy.'

'Mostly the only time we talk for that long is either in the car or on the phone. Strangely, both occasions where we don't have to make eye contact.'

Travelling together in a car provided some opportunities for communication. To the question, *How often do you talk to your Dad?*, some replies were:

'Not often. When we're in the car sometimes.'

'A lot – especially in the car ride to and from school.'

'We almost always have conversations in the car to and from school.'

'When he picks me up from school it's a twenty-minute drive, so I usually talk to him, ask how his day was and I end up listening more than talking, but it helps him so that's good.'

'I don't go out of my way to have long conversations with my dad. Occasionally me and my dad will go on drives and we'll talk then.'

Victoria, seventeen, has this to say to fathers: 'I think a good bit of advice for them would be just to be there for their daughter in whatever way they can. I think most of them would be a bit lost when it comes to boy-talks and group dramas, and aren't keen on a big heart-to-heart (that's for Mum). My stepdad's never been good with girly-talks or emotional situations, but we always go running together or do stuff in the garden, which still lets me know he's there for me and likes spending time with me.'

So many teen girls see their father as 'absent', and they're sad about it because they remember the role he played when they were younger. They remember him being more present, of always being ready to play or joke with them. But by adolescence, there's an epidemic in absenteeism. Interestingly, clinical psychologist Kirrilie Smout says that while some research existed to suggest that sheer hours of time in childhood spent with parents was not associated with better outcomes, recent research also suggested that hours of time *did* make a difference in adolescence. Parenting experts shake their heads at fathers' absences, and the girls certainly lament it. When one group of sixteen girls was asked to nominate the characteristics they wanted in the father of their children, only two answers were given, multiple times. First, the father of their children would be understanding, so that he could grasp and appreciate their children's changing lives, and second, he would spend time with his children. So did anyone in the room think their fathers gave them enough time? Silence.

Carrie is seventeen. 'As a girl who has had very little experience with fathers and only recent experience of a father-figure, I think you should remind all the fathers that, despite all the groaning and carrying on that happens when it comes to dads (especially with dad jokes and embarrassing dad comments), they are so incredibly important in their daughters' lives and they should never underestimate the influence they have.' Other girls echo this feeling.

> 'Most of the time when I call him on the phone he is either working, watching television or reading the paper. He cannot sacrifice five minutes a week to turn off the television or put the paper down to actually listen to what I am saying.'

> 'If I could ask Dad something I would ask him if we could have one night or day to do something we both love.'

These girls are calling out for more time with their fathers. They won't say it to him, but their call for it, when he's not in earshot, is loud. Not in one interview, anywhere, did a girl lament that her father did not finance overseas holidays or buy her new clothes. 'Time' was the gift they wanted, above anything. As parents, we all have the right to feel a bit robbed here. Wasn't technology supposed to deliver greater efficiency, increased productivity, a better work–life balance and a surge in leisure time? It hasn't, and families' use of technology – particularly by teen girls – along with parents' busy lives, has meant that time talking, hanging out together, going for a run or even just having dinner together is often lost. An Australian Institute of Family Studies report last year found that about one-third of all children thought their fathers worked too much. The study, called 'Long Hours and Longings'[6], revealed that 17 per cent of girls wished their father didn't have to work at all. Working weekends, being unable to vary start and stop times, and long hours all engendered negative views in children about the time demands of their fathers' work. 'The frustration felt by fathers in trying to balance work and family demands is shared by their children,' the report said.

A father's background comes to the fore here, and repeatedly girls raised it when talking about the bond they shared with their father. Some teens believed that their fathers' background was the key determiner of their parenting behaviour now. Julie, fifteen, put it this way. 'Please investigate the father's parents and how that influences his parenting. My grandma and grandad got divorced when he was about eleven and my grandma did everything for him. He now really tries to be there for me because he says his dad never was.' Or Monica: 'He talks to me because his father never talked to him.' Or Phillipa: 'The background is a big influence. Dad is really big on making sure my sister and I have a good life. He had a really hard life. He left home when he was fifteen and has been working every single day since. He's like, "You guys have to do good things. You have such a good education. You need to use it. You need to be better than I was."'

This issue of a father's background popped up often, across many issues. Girls asked me to investigate it, or whether that was the reason their father acted in a particular way. Many believed it was the single biggest factor in how their father chose to parent them.

'My father always says to us kids "I'm strict on you kids because I want you all to have what I didn't when I was younger and I want the best for you all."'

'My father is from regional Queensland and his upbringing was not as tolerant and accepting as mine, thus he can sometimes appear narrow-minded when I tell him things about my life.'

'My dad is still stuck in the life of South Africa back in the apartheid so he still worries about my safety when I walk down the road or catch a bus and won't let me be alone with a guy anywhere. He's still very old-fashioned.'

'Can you look at how they were raised and how warm/ cold their parents were to them?'

'Can you see what the impact of a father's upbringing on his own role is?'

'Neither of my parents were raised in this century or this country. My father is approaching the age of sixty-one and is clueless in this era of technology although he tries to adapt his knowledge and upgrade his iPhone each year to the latest model. When I finish school I want to study overseas but my parents said that that is not an option.'

Several mothers (more than sixty were surveyed as part of this task) also commented on their partner's background and why he parented the way he did. 'I learned a lot by seeing how he and his parents talk about and treat his sister,' one says. 'It showed me a harshness that I sometimes see him displaying with our daughter. It's not a physical thing; it's a psychological thing.' The irony of this stands out, and gives credence to the call for agility to be a strong parenting attribute. Fathers, lacking other references, are using their own parents as the yardsticks by which they deal with their own children.

Tom Matthews, who runs guidance counselling at a big school in New Zealand, says fathers can also be tied to their own experiences because they don't have the same social network that women often do in which to discuss issues. Think about this. My views are influenced by my girlfriends': those I met at university and still call my 'besties', or those I've met through work, or the mothers of my daughters' friends. My views are sometimes built through my own experience, but also through their experiences and the wisdom they offer. We talk, and parenting is frequently at the centre of those discussions – from when we should allow our daughters to engage with social media to what is the latest clothing fad. Our expectations, or how we might deal with a particular challenge, might be moulded by those discussions. Men are far less likely to do that, and the chances are that when they do – and this comes from fathers – it is highly unlikely they would devote discussion time to the latest in clothing trends. Matthews says one father recently told him that he was strict on his daughter because his own father was strict on him – but he was sure he 'wasn't half as strict as his father'. 'So his role models were very narrow,' Matthews says. 'They're not going to the pub and talking about this stuff. And even if he was, it would more likely be a disciplinary decision, where he would be supported. "You were right to throw her cell phone", or, "That's right that you did this".' Deeper conversations were unlikely. In short, it was the way his father parented him that could become the sole influence on how he then treated his own daughter. 'Women will talk through their issues a lot more.

So by default, their role models become more broad,' he says. John Gray, author of *Men are from Mars, Women are from Venus*, agrees. 'Conditioning is everything,' he says. 'What you saw as a child is what you automatically do as an adult, and the only way that changes is if you are consciously brought to see that what your parents did doesn't work.'

Tim, the father of three girls aged eleven, thirteen and fifteen, agrees. 'I had a father who was a doctor who was away for hours and hours at a time. I've always tried to have a job where I've got time through the day for the kids,' he says. His father was absent; he's determined not to be. Of course, many fathers don't have that option. Family finances or work requirements demand they are away for long days, or even days at a time. But there is no doubt, girls believe, that it comes at a cost to them – unless the time can be made up in other ways. One school principal says she's noticed, in recent years, fathers stopping by a coffee shop with their daughters before they drop them to school. They might be squeezing in only twenty minutes, but it was twenty minutes, *alone*, with their daughter. And it frequently makes her day. Tim says he also made the decision to choose activities he could share with his family. 'I don't go and play golf anymore. We either do it as a family or we don't do it. I do think it comes down to your relationship with your own parents and you decide, "that's not what I'm going to do". That's made the difference to me.'

Just one more note on a father's background, because it plays a role rarely discussed. It surfaced several times, in relation to fathers who make the decision to come to Australia to enhance their children's future. 'You can't stereotype,' one principal says, 'but we would certainly see that with many Asian girls.' In these cases, the girls have sought help from the school because of the expectations put on them, and the lack of time for anything else, including time spent with their parents. These girls might be required to perform well at school, go to outside tutoring to assist with their studies, and play the violin to a high level. 'It's very regimented and I think the girls who struggle the most with that is where we've seen it is very dogmatic.'

Julie Feeney, a Victorian deputy principal, says family time is also being chewed up by long commutes to feeder schools that cater for students across big cities. In addition, extracurricular activities mean some girls leave home before 7 am and do not return until after 7 pm. This poses a challenge to parents wanting to engage more with their children. Experts suggest families schedule into their diary 'family time' each week. That gives it a priority, providing children with 'a voice in the family' and potentially giving each child prime responsibility for something specific. Feeney says that, for girls, this would add both value to her identity and illustrate her value within the family. Educationalist and former principal Dr Tim Hawkes says circumstances might dictate that fathers struggle with allocating a significant quantity of time to his family – but that shouldn't rule out quality time. 'The time they do have is not time to hide behind the newspaper, not time to stalk off somewhere thinking "this is my time", not a time to get stuck into the beer and watch the telly and zone out while they self-medicate on what might have been a pretty demanding day,' he says. When fathers come home from work – no matter what is going on there – they have to be in 'fathering mode, not recovery mode'. Dr Hawkes would like to remind each father that as his daughter dozes off to sleep her mind will continue to work on what last occupied it. If it was a conversation with her father, his influence could be profound. 'If, on the other hand, Lucy has just facetimed her or Bill has just told her she's got a face like a pizza, that's what's going to be in her mind,' he says. He is unapologetic on this issue, and you can hear the frustration build in his voice. 'The legitimate question can be asked, who is it who is raising your daughter?' He says a fourteen- to sixteen-year-old girl might spend two to five hours in front of a screen daily – and that means that becomes a bigger influence on her in some cases than her parents. 'More than once I've had parents come to me and say, "Well, I don't know where they've picked up this dreadful habit from. It certainly wasn't from me" and I feel like saying, "You're absolutely right. I don't think they've picked up much from you at all!"'

If fathers were clued in on the effect of long absences on their daughters, it would almost certainly change the absenteeism the girls describe. That certainly was the case for Christopher. 'I was told two or three years ago that I needed to become more present in my daughter's life – I had never realised I was not giving that to her – and have worked hard since to give her as much time as I can, and I think she has been helped by my doing that.' Brisbane GP Dr Steve Hambleton says his personal experience shows that too. During the three-year period he served as federal president of the Australian Medical Association, he wasn't home often. Meetings, flights to Canberra, strategy workshops, media commitments. He'd always worked long hours, but he then found himself away more than he was at home, and it coincided with the period in which one of his daughters was transitioning into adulthood. Did it really matter? His answer is immediate. 'It had a huge impact on her development, and the impact on the family is extraordinary,' he says.

For years, the effects of separation and divorce on children have been mulled over by researchers, academics and psychologists. A unanimity of views exist that a child's academic performance might plummet, along with her self-esteem, and behavioural problems can flourish in homes where children live without a father or father-figure. Divorce and daughters is discussed in the next chapter, but what about the impact of 'fly-in, fly-out dads'? Fathers who work overseas, or interstate. Fathers who run businesses that require travel. Or those who work in the same town or city as their family but who spend all waking hours away? Educators say they can often spot when a girl's father is not at home. One principal, who works in a region that services itinerant workforces, says that when a mother arrives at her office to talk about an issue involving a daughter, 'the chances are Dad will be away or posted overseas and not at home at that time'. That should be evidence to fathers, she says, of their vital role in keeping their daughter grounded. Of course, this doesn't include those families who are fatherless. Throughout this project, experts talk of fathers or father-figures – other good role models who demonstrate the attributes of good men.

Tom Matthews says that, from his experience, most father–daughter relationship breakdowns are caused by fathers being absent or inconsistent. 'I see these kids – it's almost like they've got this fragile gift to put out there and have all this desire to hang out with their dads, and then it just gets crushed when their dads don't turn up or even when they're late sometimes,' he says. Girls put enormous stock in their fathers turning up – even when they don't have a strong relationship. 'I don't know why it is,' Matthews says. 'It's almost hardwired sometimes. It's as though the girls get hungry for that connection and really sensitive when it is not there.' Adelaide principal Kevin Tutt says younger girls, before the onset of adolescence, can be particularly affected by absent fathers. That's the time, he says, when they are wanting to taste independence from their mothers but need a hearty dose of close-by support.

So what is the impact of an AWOL father? Shelford Girls' Grammar's Polly Flanagan says you could 'almost see it', and there was 'almost a tangible difference' between girls who had a consistent male figure in their lives, and, in some cases, those who didn't. Let me emphasise the 'some cases', because it is an important qualification. An 'absent father' affects girls differently, depending on their resilience and age and a host of other variables. Flanagan says most schools hosted some students who had never met, or known, their fathers. In some cases their fathers had died; in other cases custody rested with someone else. 'I remember a couple of enrolment forms and there's one side for the mother's details and one for the father's – and the father's side had been crossed out, as if he didn't exist.' But while the effect of an absent dad varies, she says a closeness between father and daughter shines brightly. 'It's very difficult for any family – particularly attending schools where the fees are reasonably high and there's an imperative that there be a double income to support that

– to not feel stretched as a family,' she says. 'And families are pushed and pushed and pushed and I think there are some who make time for their kids, who do things with their kids, and I think that matters. It's really important that you're not just there in the family home, because you can actually be an absent father and live with the kids.'

What concerns Barker College's Phillip Heath is his belief that sons and daughters are both affected by 'absent dads or overburdened dads or dads who are present but aren't really present'. But here's his specific concern about girls: it might be more difficult to notice the impact. 'The girls tend to – to the outward world – find ways to manage that better than the boys do,' he says. 'You might find a boy will do something to insist Dad takes notice; the girl not so much. The girl . . . she makes do.' He says 'present' fathers are able to instil in their daughters a confidence, at the intuitive level, by giving them a voice. Jennifer Oaten, principal of Santa Maria College in Perth, says fathers also provide a different daily perspective on issues ranging from clothing to public events, and that could give girls a solid grounding. As to whether fathers understand that their daughters want more time with them, she says, 'I think many of them are unaware, and I don't think men quite realise how much their daughters value that time with them; how special it is for them.' She gives the example of school camp for Years 5 and 6, which fills up quickly each year. 'That's because the girls are driving it, not the dads. They're the ones saying, "Dad, I want you to go, I want you to sign up!"' Other principals say similar things. With father–daughter dances for older girls, the students love them and push their fathers to attend, often arranging tables on their behalf. 'The girls are the ones wanting to dance; sometimes it's the dads who don't,' one principal says.

Perhaps the answer, then, is to encourage our girls to nurture other connections with their fathers? That question is politely batted away each time I ask. Girls should play their part, they say, but the onus lies with their fathers 'turning up'. Dr Justin Coulson, a parenting expert with six daughters, says that we make time for those things in our lives we really value. 'Every dad I talk to says, "I value my daughter or children, my family is the most important thing in my life."' Then when the families are falling apart and they review their calendar, there's no time in their calendar for family! They do have time for everything else. Work is a given, but they do make time for their favourite show on the telly and they do make time for their exercise or recreation, or time out with the boys.' He finishes with this warning: 'Squeaky wheels get oil, and teenagers stop being squeaky because they've got friends and devices and other things to keep them going.'

Absent dads might find it difficult to move back into their daughters' lives later on, too. The rationale for that is that the foundation of closeness and trust and easy conversation needs to be bedded down, before girls go down the tunnel of adolescence. Jennifer Oaten says that, particularly in difficult times, daughters will be drawn back to their fathers if they have spent valuable time with them earlier. 'They know Dad's always there. They know they can talk to him about anything and everything. But you need to build that relationship – the dad–daughter relationship – not when they're fifteen or sixteen because that's too late. You need to be building it much earlier.' Calrossy Anglican School's principal David Smith says, 'You get one crack at being a parent,' and he is not alone in voicing frustration that fathers are not as involved with their daughters as their mothers. 'We don't want to diminish the importance of fathers in the lives of girls,' he says. Finding the time can be difficult, but it needs to be a priority. 'One of the most fun things I ever did with my kids was to teach them how to drive. I have parents say, "Oh, it's 120 hours; it's such a pain in the neck!" I say, 120 hours in a car with a kid where you talk!'

Tim has three daughters and he says he has ups and downs on a daily basis, like most parents. But he says he is a rare beast on school grounds, and always has been. He's always taken his girls to the class door, and nodded at the teacher. Rarely, he says, has he run into other men doing the same. That is, at least, until special events like Father's Day. 'You'd come to Father's Day and there would be all these dads saying, "What's this", "Where's this room?" "Where do we have to be?"' It's a salient warning. Giving daughters time when they are young is the prerequisite for receiving it later.

10

Separated families

'Dad, why did you leave?' Those are the specific five words many girls said they wanted to ask, given the opportunity. But so many other questions have also sat unanswered as their parents split, divorce and move on. Is it Mum's fault or your fault? they want to ask. Or perhaps it's my fault? Why did you/Mum act that way? Who will I live with? Why won't you tell me anything? Where will you/Mum go? Will we be able to stay at our school? Will you/Mum marry your new girlfriend/ boyfriend? Will I have to move away from my friends? Will my sister and I be separated? If only I had been easier to get along with, maybe this might not have happened. Perhaps it really *is* my fault.

It's not just heartache that's at the centre of the family home when a decision is made to separate. That, of itself, is a gargantuan decision, brought on after months or years of consideration. It might follow a breakdown in communication or loyalty or trust, and for each parent it will lead to some anguish, sadness and perhaps anger too. Sometimes the adults at the centre of that decision will struggle to cope. That puts into perspective the difficulty for any children in the relationship.

Often divorce works for parents. They are happier, able to move on and in many cases remarry. Sometimes it works for children, too, and they skate through the period without feeling particularly unsettled. But what needs to happen for it to work for children? The answer to that question is vital, because so many girls say they feel forced to take a side, or they lose contact with one parent, or worry that they are to blame. Many of them are confused and angry, even years later. Experts warn that some of the consequences of divorce can follow them through life, leading to low self-esteem, a difficulty in setting a moral compass, and an inability to create solid priorities in life. They have to navigate between two parents, often playing them off against each other. These girls pique the concern of those who see it. 'They become a pawn in a game,' one principal said. 'It's really, really tough,' another said. 'My heart bleeds when you pick up a student whose parents are really adversarial,' says a third. 'It's absolutely devastating. You just want them to pull together for the benefit of their daughter.'

Indeed, that's what girls say they want, particularly when they are younger. They want Mum and Dad to reunite. They admit to setting out to dislike their parents' new partners. They want what they used to have. 'I don't talk to my stepmum,' Eliza says. 'She's not my mother.' 'Your dad and stepfather compete for your emotions all the time,' another says. 'It's really hard. I have to go back and forth all the time,' says a twelve-year-old. It doesn't work, often, for one or both parents either. 'My daughter's mother and I separated over two years ago,' Russ says. 'Unfortunately it came as a massive shock to me and I didn't take it very well. The children suffered a bit as a result of it all. My daughter has chosen to stay with her mum because of things that she has been told which are very untrue.'

In some cases it does work, however, and Brigid, fifteen, puts it down – in her case – to mirror rules being enacted at both her mother's and her father's house. 'I'll go two weeks with Mum without seeing Dad, and then two weeks with Dad and not seeing Mum. They have a great relationship. But you really depend on that one when you're with them. That's why it works.' It even helped Tania's relationship with her father. 'My parents separated, thus sparking dual custody. It has meant I am spending significantly more one-on-one time with Dad and as a result it has made us closer and has enabled us to relate to each other.' Ally feels the same. 'I believe that we have gotten closer now that I am older and understand more about the world. He is more real with me and we have more we can relate to.' Or Kellie, who says she knows that if she fell, her stepfather 'would be there to pick me up'. So many of her friends feel otherwise, penning heartbreaking and fragile tributes to the parent they don't see, outlining their anger at being rebuffed and wondering what else they, as teenagers, need to do to have two parents. Many of them have already concluded, by their mid-teens, that there is nothing else they can do.

'I can't do more because he's the one who ended all ties with the family.'

'He hurt me too much and took our family house. Left us with nothing.'

'I have tried everything to have a better connection with him. I gave up because he wanted to be with his wife.'

'I never see him to tell him that I miss him.'

'Mum doesn't like me talking to him or seeing him.'

'I could try and be nice to his girlfriend?'

'I don't need to improve anything. He needs to pick up his act and stop being a bitch to my mother.'

One in four Australian children live in one-parent families, and in the vast majority of cases they live with their mother. In this survey, 80 per cent of those whose parents separated remained with their mother. The girls were open and honest about what they wanted their father to do.

'To try to keep in contact and not treat my mother as an enemy.'

'Call more. He didn't even remember that my semi-formal was this week.'

'Pay my school fees and help my mum pay for us.'

'Ring every now and again.'

'I want him to want to see me.'

'Come to my house more often and see what I'm doing and if I want to do something with him.'

'Come over just because he wants to see us. He actually told us once, not even caring that it might hurt our feelings, that he went to three of his friends' places more than he came to our house.'

'Talk to me more, not just ring every blue moon.'

Mothers have a role here too, because if it's accepted that children benefit from good communication between parents, wouldn't it be possible for a mother to encourage that communication, or remind her ex-partner that a semi-formal is around the corner? In some cases those efforts are rebuffed, no matter how hard one party might try. But it's inevitable that no contact means any chasm in the relationship between girls and the adult they do not live with grows. Because (at least in this survey) the majority of girls lived with their mothers, that gulf was in the relationship between them and their fathers.

'We don't see each other as much anymore because I live with Mum most of the time.'

'It feels a bit strained because of what has happened with me moving but all in all I love him very much.'

'As I get older he is less and less a part of my life. I only see him on birthdays and at Christmas.'

'The last time I saw my dad was four or five years ago. And the last time he sent me a letter was three years ago.'

'I only see him every three months. He has stopped giving me presents on my birthday.'

'My mum divorced my dad when I was three. When he got married to his new wife she turned him against me.'

'After I stopped going to his house he stopped making an effort with me. The only way he could understand my life was through three-minute phone calls, which

is almost impossible. He also stopped coming to my sporting matches or music performances, the things that were really important to me.'

Social researcher Mark McCrindle draws our attention to a silver lining in the clouds brought on by divorce. Rates are declining and have continued to decline over the past decade. Couples are marrying later in life, with more money and maturity behind them. Most couples with dependent children have two incomes. 'That shows mums are earning money and dads are earning money, and if there's a relational split, there's not so much of a financial reliance of one party over another.' Couples are also divorcing either before children come along, or at an older age, he adds. 'While it is still going to impact teenagers, it's not growing,' he says. 'For the first time, the number of divorces where children are involved is dropping. In terms of numbers and children involved, it is less of an issue than it might have been in the past.' In number terms it looks like this. In 2016, 46 604 divorces were granted, a drop of almost 4 per cent on the previous year. The Australian Bureau of Statistics also reports that divorces involving children represented 49.9 per cent of all divorces, also slightly down on the previous year. But the number of children involved in divorces still totalled more than 40 000 in 2016.[7] A rider needs to be included here: divorce rates don't capture de facto couple separation rates, and they are more likely to separate compared with married couples – even when they have children. One-third of children in recent years were born outside marriage, and most of those were to de facto couples. Children living with cohabitating parents were twice as likely as those living with married parents to experience parental separation.

It's worth remembering here that no two families are the same, and as said already, some will pass through their parents' divorce totally unscathed. Seymour College principal Kevin Tutt says often the challenge presented to a family by a divorce is mirrored by other challenges faced by families. 'I could cite examples here of girls who spent 50 per cent of their time between Mum and Dad, or every second weekend with Dad – and they are managing really well,' he says. 'Indeed, if you didn't know their family circumstances, you would never guess it.' He then tells of a challenge involving another family, whose father died when his daughter was eight. 'I interviewed her . . . and she just talked about how much she misses him – that connection with the most important man in her life.' It's how these challenges are dealt with that can make all the difference.

'I've learnt to be independent,' Julia, thirteen, says. And Ellie, fourteen, says, 'I enjoy my own company now.' 'I grew up very, very quickly,' says Danni, aged fifteen. Teachers agree. Independence, an ability to look after themselves, a quick maturity even 'a thick skin' can follow for a girl whose parents separate. Girls also say that they feel better, sometimes, because the bickering and yelling between their parents has stopped. They no longer have to avoid them or hide in their room, pretending not to hear. While on the surface that might be preferable, it also brings to the fore an issue some school leaders raised, and that is how quickly our teens are being forced to grow up (divorce being just one of the factors influencing that). Mark McCrindle calls this age group the 'up-agers' because they are older, younger – a gift provided by modern technology. From an educational point of view, that can be of enormous benefit. Remember sitting down to do an assignment with the A–Z of the *Encyclopaedia Britannica* by your side? That can now be done with more efficiency – and depth – with the click of a couple of buttons. But technology also brings risks. The availability of porn, a culture that is turning children into adults and girls into women, years before they should. This is a worry articulated across the board: that these factors are forcing our children to grow up prematurely. 'They are children for such a short space of time,' says Polly Flanagan, principal of Shelford Girls' Grammar. 'Some children are robbed of a childhood, I think; they are mini adults by the time they are twelve.' While her comments are not specifically focused on divorce, this is what girls whose parents are divorced describe when talking about their new-found 'independence'. Flanagan has taken to talking about growing up too early at school assemblies. 'Enjoy being a child,' she tells her students. 'Once you are an adult, behaving like a child is not a pretty thing. Once you reach adulthood, you are in that zone for the rest of your life.'

Sometimes, in divorces, parents succeed in not criticising each other in front of their children. But often the children become the rope in a tug of war. They see and hear arguments they should not have to at the age of five or ten or twelve or sixteen. But that's just the beginning, for some families. 'I've had mothers in here in tears saying he's got a new partner and now won't pay half the fees,' says the principal of a private school. Some girls say they are forced to move schools 'because Dad won't pay the fees'. 'All the while, the child is at the centre,' another principal says. 'I think it suppresses some children and they become incredibly quiet, but you can almost tell with those children. They are looking around, and they've got this adult surveillance about them.' Fathers are not always the perpetrators of problems here; many of those without custody of their daughters tell of the heartache of seeking contact and more involvement, but being shunned. Experts advise fathers in that situation to just keep trying. 'It's human nature, when you get hurt and rejected and pushed away and told you're not wanted, to back off,' Kirrilie Smout says. 'It takes incredible courage for a parent to say, "I hear you and I respect your independence but I am going to be in your life as much as I possibly can." That courage pays off in the long term.'

Dr Tim Hawkes, former headmaster of The King's School in Parramatta, Sydney, doesn't mince words, saying a family break-up can be one of the greatest problems and worries for teenage girls. 'The reality is, there is almost a perfect correlation in my schools that I've been teaching at or where I've had the privilege of leading . . . between a troubled student who is behaviourally reprehensible, and strife and trouble at home in terms of the relationship between parents.' He says that's not to say that this was always the case, or that unhappy marriages shouldn't be dissolved. Of course it wasn't. But he says 'the flotsam and jetsam of a disintegrating family washes up on schools', adding, 'But more importantly, it washes up on children and can lead to all sorts of problems.'

Research has repeatedly illustrated what those problems can be. A lack of confidence. A drop in self-esteem. Young girls becoming sexually active too early. Teachers sometimes see girls' academic performances plummet, and troubles erupt in their friendship groups. Overwhelmingly, experts say, this happens in cases where parents do not put their child's wellbeing at the centre of their decisions. 'The consequences can be huge and confusing for an individual student,' one principal said. 'They can end up having to navigate – and, dare I say it, manipulate, albeit subconsciously – relationships and navigate between two parents. It can be incredibly difficult.'

Certainly the girls admit that they can play one parent off against the other to benefit themselves – and not only when their parents are divorcing!

> 'They're divorced, so if I'm arguing with one I'll go to the other one, who will usually take my side.'

> 'If I'm arguing with my mum, I'll make it out to Dad that Mum is doing the wrong thing. They don't really talk to each other, they relay information through me.'

> 'I'll just tell Dad that Mum has already said yes, and I'll tell Mum that Dad said it was fine. They are both competing to be my favourite. Easy.'

A layer of difficulty, or at the very least complexity, arises during custody battles or once one parent finds a new partner.

> 'Anything I really say to my dad that is even slightly negative about my experience at Mum's house he will use in court.'

> 'We were close when I was younger but ever since he's gotten with another "significant other". He's changed into someone he's not.'

'I wish I could spend some time with just him, without my stepmum and half-brother and sisters around, because I never have in my life.'

Educators see it often. Former New Zealand principal Gillian Simpson says one of the most damaging acts a parent – man or woman – can do is to use their daughter against their former partner. She, like others, has seen it at school where 'the father sort of uses the daughter to get back at the mother in some way – emotionally or financially – and that's incredibly damaging for the girls. In the end, a lot of dads miss out.' Sometimes it's the other way around, too, and experts say the girls cope with this by trying to 'look after everybody' in the situation. 'They want to mother Dad and mother Mum, and they get ripped apart by it,' Gillian Simpson says. 'It's awful.' Linda Douglas, another principal, says: 'Those girls become Switzerland, sometimes, because if the landscape is not a pleasant one, they can be caught in the middle too. Not only are they trying to seek support, they're trying to smooth the landscape between two parties for their own interest. Who equips a fourteen-year-old girl to do that?'

School guidance specialist Tom Matthews says a starting point is for parents to understand that when they separate, their children can routinely believe it is their fault. That might be their default position. 'You've got to actively counter that bias,' he says. 'You've got to sit them down and tell them it is not their fault.' And you have to do that repeatedly. 'The only way to break through that is when they see that the relationship is still functioning, even though they are not living together.' Principal Polly Flanagan says it's important for both parents to 'just keep talking' to their daughters. That's so important because a separation might be only one issue a girl is dealing with; she might also be beset with friendship problems, or difficulties at school, or caught up in social media. She feels as though she cannot approach either parent. While once upon a time it was a punishment to say to a child, 'Go to your room', now it sits there like an invitation. 'Just keep talking,' she says. 'It's connect, connect and connect, and find a way of connecting. Whether it's taking them to the footy or a ballet lesson, whether it's a cooking class or a meal cooked together once a week, or every Sunday afternoon you do X, Y and Z – but you've got to connect because there are lots of forces in society that make really happy-together families disconnect.'

Dr Briony Scott from Wenona supports what many of the girls are saying about wanting to keep both parents in their lives. 'Even if parents divorce,' she says, 'you don't get the luxury or the right to no longer be involved. That unconditional strand is there, even if you choose to ignore it.' Dr Scott says both parents can feel the heartache caused by a separation, or something else going dreadfully wrong in a family. 'I have an equal number of men and women who come into my office and just sob,' she says. 'We understand a woman's grief; we don't always understand the man's grief, and it's real.' That's so true, and father after father has detailed their own anguish at a marriage breakdown, and often what they see as the 'loss' of their children. 'I'd like to see more of her but her mother won't allow it' is a common refrain. Others believe they have been 'shut out'. They aren't told about the daily ups and downs their daughters are navigating, so they can't deepen their relationship. Still others made these comments:

'I would love for her to stay with my wife and me more often.'

'I'm separated from her mother. They have different values to me and run their lives very differently. I would like to support her in building the foundations of an independent, successful life and the behaviours that support that. She doesn't want to address things like that with me, and her mother doesn't support what I think is important. Very difficult for a father to do much in this situation.'

'I would like my daughter to stop being alienated from me by her mother. I would like her to ask me questions on schoolwork, and I would like her to spend time with me, and my friends, without constantly sulking with the attitude of "why do I have to be here?"'

Researcher and writer Linda Nielsen, a professor of educational and adolescent psychology at Wake Forest University, wrote in *The Conversation* that research had shown that daughters' relationships with their fathers were more damaged than sons'. 'What's more, estranged daughters are more likely than estranged sons to suffer negative effects from the damaged relationship,' she says. Mothers were also able to pass on negative impressions of their partners without speaking – through 'the expressions on her face, her tone of voice, the way she acts after she's talked to him or when you're going to spend time with him'. 'Unfortunately, this happens to millions of daughters – especially when Dad has remarried but Mum is still single.' Professor Nielsen says the more often her mother implied her father was to blame, the more difficult it was for a daughter to have an open mind about him.[8]

Children can lose in a divorce. So can fathers. And mothers too. Girls routinely express bitterness, anger, sadness and frustration that, despite trying, some fathers had closed the door and moved on. 'I've given up,' Cathy told me. He comes in and out of her life and doesn't think about what that does to her. 'Now I just try to ensure he has as little contact as possible.' The bottom line is that without a commitment to communicating with each other, and keeping children at the centre of their discussions, few examples surface of a divorce working – at least for the child. Sometimes the effort to make it work is extraordinary. But in Alex's view, well worth it. 'I think I am rare, having grown up myself the youngest of four raised by a single dad, so I have a strong sense of commitment to parenting and have the kind of honest relationship with my daughter that many parents would envy,' he says. 'I have also co-parented her since six weeks of age with her mother, whom I split with, and have moved cities and jobs to be close to her, as her mother has moved twenty-three times in those fourteen years, and she's gone to seven schools. I spent every birthday and Christmas until she was twelve sharing that day with her Mum and I together so that our family unit existed in spite of our break-up.' Not every non-custodian parent can go to that effort, but being on the same page is certainly a good start. 'I am a child of divorced parents,' says a mother, Yvonne. 'I was three when they separated. While I have always maintained a close relationship with my father and his side of the family (I am now forty-four), I realised as an adult what an anomaly I am – especially with the presence of a stepfather in my life for thirty-five years. Sadly, many fathers often just drift out of their children's lives, and as a parent, I don't know how this can happen. I would love to see this explored. Are there certain "qualities" that make a father maintain contact, or is it circumstantial? Have patterns changed over the last thirty years?'

Certainly separation is now easier, helped by both the law and women's increased participation in the workforce. But the 'qualities' Yvonne asks about come down to communication and a willingness to make it work, say the experts. 'The most important thing for parents,' Associate Professor Michael Nagel says, 'is that they have to be on the same team, and it's really important for kids to see that. We know that kids of all ages will play parents off one another, given the opportunity, and they're good at reading it. It's really really important for Mum and Dad to be on the same page and have a proactive plan of attack,' he says. Additionally, children don't blame themselves, he says, when families work through a separation peacefully, and the children know their love for them is both unconditional and constant. It doesn't become us versus them – Mum's side or Dads' side, he says.

A teen girl has a tower of issues to confront, and her best chance of toppling it is with the support of adult role models – male and female – who have her wellbeing at the centre of their decision-making. Cassie is one of many girls going to school this morning. 'My parents have separated and the process hasn't exactly been smooth ... I'm sad to say he's no longer a part of my life anymore.' Or this from Jessie: 'I'd like to tell my dad how much I love him and how grateful I am for him. I also would want to tell him that although he has his new wife and two new kids, he needs to try and show love to his own kids when we feel left out.' That's not too much to ask, is it?

11

Sons and daughters

Sally, fifteen, reckons her father, an SAS-trained defence-force dad, is odds-on favourite to win the 'Most Over-protective Father Award'. 'He says he is prepared to use force against any partner of mine,' she tells her friends. 'He's told me they [the SAS] will be following him or anyone else he doesn't know.' She stops for just a moment. Her group of fifteen or so friends is listening to every word. 'I assume he's joking. I think.' Tanya, fourteen, says her father could top that. 'My dad will let me catch the train into the city, and I think that's cool, and then I learnt he's actually tracking my phone,' she says. Her disbelief is shared. 'One time – I live two streets away from Coles – I went down to get something for dinner. My phone died, which meant Dad couldn't track it anymore.' Tanya says she was away for less than ten minutes. 'He got into the car and started searching the streets around Coles. He thought I'd been picked up by someone!'

Each one of these girls has her own story; a story in which she thinks her father's actions to protect her are disproportionate to what was needed, and out of whack with how her father would treat her brother. Jemima says, 'If I say I'm going to walk around the corner to a friend's house, he goes "Where? Which one? Why? Can't I drive you?"' She says that before she can argue her case he has his keys in his hand and is heading for the car to drive her the 400 metres to her friend's home. Bronnie says, 'I say I'll be back in two minutes and he still wants to drive me!' She laments that her father won't practise what he preaches. 'My dad is from South Africa and has all these stories,' she says. 'He didn't steal stuff, but did some stuff. But I say, "I'll take the dog for a walk" and he says, "No no no no!" He is so over-protective – but when he was my age he did what he wanted.' Chloe goes to the nub of the issue of fathers struggling to allow their daughters independence: 'My dad barely lets me leave the house without parental supervision,' she says. 'It's hard to talk to him about the stuff going down at school, or how the guy at the bus stop was staring at me. I can't even express my opinions that I strongly support without him going "Awww, that's my little baby girl." It makes me feel small and weak.'

Maddy. Emily. Emma. Annie. Claudia. Their names differ, and so do their schools, but their tales bear remarkable similarities – as does the interpretation of what those stories mean to the girls. Fathers are over-protective because they see their daughters as unable to look after themselves in the same way a boy their age – or their brother – could. 'He says times are different,' Emily says. Indeed, some fathers, looking back in time, admit their protective streak comes from remembering what *they* were like at that age, and worrying that their daughters might find themselves mixing with boys who thought like them. 'My father says "look where it led me" – but I'm not him,' Rachel says. And Brigid, seventeen, tells of how her father just doesn't want her to grow up. 'He wanted me to be a kid as far as I could. He said to live in the moment, but he kept wanting me to be that age forever.'

The girls believe their father parents by gender. They believe they are treated differently *because* they are girls. That means their fathers see them as 'more vulnerable', 'not as strong', 'weaker' than their brothers. 'My father trusts my brothers more in the outside world,' says Kylie. 'He believes that they can look after themselves.' This view permeated the girls' answers, along with a belief that their fathers wanted 'tougher' sons, found it easier to deal with boys, and shared a bond with their brothers that they struggled to enjoy with them. It wasn't that their fathers were less ambitious for them, it was just that they didn't treat them as equals.

'When my brother leaves for boarding school Dad says, "Off you go", and when I go he actually cries!'

'He prefers them and congratulates their efforts and praises them and brags about them. He does not care about me.'

'They seem to talk more and go out for breakfast to talk once a week.'

'It's like Dad and my brothers, and me, my sister and my mum. Like it's divided into the boys and the girls.'

'Even the way Dad talks to us – me and my brother – is different. It's easy-breezy with me and really strict with Thomas.'

'My brother is a bit soft so dad tries to toughen him up.'

The girls are articulate and passionate and definite in their answers . . . and they're also willing to diagnose *why* their father acts in this way. In many cases, they believe it is a mutual interest in sport that provides a packet-mix bond for father and son.

'He's more protective with me than my brothers. When I started going through puberty, he just went more to the boys and their sport. He'd talk to them about that now.'

'My relationship is different with my dad than my brother's relationship is with him, because Dad does more activities with my brother, like surf club and soccer.'

'My dad and my brother connect over soccer. I know my dad loves me a lot. It's not that he prefers my brother, but he has more of a connection [with my brother]. He goes to my sport, too, but it's mainly my brother. They have it in common.'

'He does fun activities with my brother that I'm not involved in.'

'My brother relates more to my dad because he has the same hobbies.'

'My brother is closer to Dad because he's the sporty one in the family.'

With that rationale, it shouldn't come as a surprise to learn that those girls who believe their father parents them in a similar fashion to their brothers nominate sport as the 'connector'. This was particularly the case where their chosen pastime was a sport their father also played, or followed. Hockey, basketball, swimming, running and AFL popped up. Their father either drove them to training, coached them or was a passionate supporter of a team at a higher level. Some girls even pondered whether increasing their sporting activity might grab more of their father's attention. 'I don't really think there is anything more I can do except do more swimming, like my brother – even though I do four and a half hours a week already,' Alison says.

Fathers don't flinch at the suggestion that they parent their sons and daughters in diverse ways. They agree. Here is a snapshot of answers to the question, *If you have a son, is there a difference in how you parent him, compared to your daughter?*

'Yes. I expect different things from him than I do from our girls.'

'Yes, because my son and I share interests (especially sporting ones) that my wife and daughter do not share with us.'

'Yes, because he is a boy, I am less protective.'

'There's always more to worry about with a daughter!'

'I am going to look after my daughter more than our son because she is a girl and may need more support and protection.'

'I am much harder on my eleven-year-old son and I really don't have an answer as to why. Maybe I want him to take on more of my characteristics.'

'Yes, I probably don't let him cry as much as I would allow my daughter.'

'Yes, probably. We do some more boy stuff and he loves the rough and tumble. He needs to be able to look after himself.'

Fathers claim their sons are subject to both stronger discipline and greater freedom. They say they jump to the defence of their daughters before their sons, particularly during sibling play, like a pool fight. They try to ensure the division of household duties is even, although it is more likely their son would do work outside the home – from washing the car to mowing the lawn. Often, they say, the divergence in parenting is a response to the way their children behave.

'I try to treat them the same when I can but I have to walk on eggshells when dealing with my daughter.'

'I tend to do different activities with my sons, more outdoor-focused. They enjoy being in the bush/four-wheel driving, whereas my daughter enjoys less risky activities.'

'He is more resilient and less likely to hold grudges.'

*'He's less volatile than my daughter so our relationship
is less volatile.'*

That honesty is revealing, and perhaps a touch alarming
too. But girls, at least in this survey, *expect* that they
will be treated differently. Some say the relationship
their brothers share with their fathers simply mirrors the
relationship they have with their mothers. 'My brother
and my father are closer but that's okay because I am
very close with my mother,' one says. 'My brother and
father spend a lot more time together,' offers another.
'My brother is clearly Dad's favourite. Their relationship
is quite similar to the relationship I have with my mum.'
Ange says she misses out, because she has to compete
with her brothers for time with her father. 'Since I have
three brothers, he spends more time with them. I think
the time we have together is too busy and rushed to talk.'

The chief impetus to complain about the difference in
treatment only comes when girls are in their mid-teens
and seeking greater independence. That's when they butt
heads with their father's determination to 'protect' them.
To many girls it signals a distrust, at one end, and misogyny at the other. 'Why do fathers feel the need to be
so protective of their daughters but not their sons?' one
girl asked. Or this from a fifteen-year-old: 'I feel so many
fathers are misogynistic, homophobic. We need to see more
dads educating their sons better so more fathers will be

more understanding and free of toxic masculinity.' And this: 'Do dads generally have expectations for careers for their sons and motherhood for the daughters? To what extent does the man still believe in the conservative '50s domestic ideals?'

So how do educators read this? For many, it is high on their list of concerns. Dr Julie Wilson Reynolds, from St Hilda's on the Gold Coast, sums up the disquiet of several experts, who see a new protectionism limiting girls' ability to judge risk, develop critical thinking skills and even just live life. 'The over-protective father can really damage the self-efficacy of his daughter,' she says. 'I think dads can be tempted to ride in and fight the dragons and fix everything for his distressed daughter. He just has to see her in tears and he wants to fix it.'

Generalisations are difficult to escape in looking at all dads and all daughters, even if there are strong common threads and themes in how they think. Some dads are not over-protective, and welcome their daughters' journey to independence. Others are not in their daughters' lives at all. Others are protective outside school but leave what goes on between 8 am and 4 pm entirely in the hands of school. Some mothers are also more protective than their partners. But in this research task, all those were excep-tions to a general rule – that fathers were overwhelmingly more protective. 'It's weird,' Tarnya, fifteen, says. 'Dad is really chilled at home. I can go in the pool by myself, stay up late, watch Netflix and Mum is always on my case. Then it comes to going out, and Mum is okay, while Dad wants a risk assessment for every ten minutes I'm out!' Certainly, inside the school grounds mothers are more likely to be advocating for their child, or checking on her welfare. It is only when the problem escalates that fathers will routinely become involved. Two principals offer that fathers might also display that same advocacy with their sons, but are generally less inclined to get involved – it's for their daughters they want the path cleared.

Among educators, the term coined to describe this is 'snowplough parenting', and it refers to parents who want to race ahead of their child and make the road all straight and smooth. Micro-managing their lives, they might have their breakfast on the table when they wake them, and fill their child's schedule with tutorials to give them a better chance at their studies. They want nothing to go wrong, so they spend their time countering obstacles that might pop up each day. Examples given vary from fathers coaching teams so that their daughter is chosen for a sport, to mothers doing her assignments.

If experts exist who suggest doing tasks like these for your daughter is beneficial, I couldn't find them. Indeed, the experts warned against it, because the message given to a girl is that she cannot do it herself. Dr Julie Wilson Reynolds says, 'I have sat in this very office and talked to parents – mums and dads – and said, "What do you think your daughter is hearing when you say you've come into the school to fix this for her?"' Dr Wilson Reynolds says the response is always along the lines of 'What do you mean "what is she hearing"? We just want to fix it.' But she says that while 'fixing it' is what parents might voice to their daughter, she is more likely to hear that she cannot do it by herself. Dr Wilson Reynolds tells parents this: 'You are actually damaging her own self-belief and her connection with you, because she then feels you don't believe she can do it. And that will discourage her.' Principals and teen psychologists nominate over-protectionism as one of the biggest risks in parenting because, they say, the effects can last a lifetime. Dr Wilson Reynolds says it risks having a generational impact. 'It will impact the girls' self-belief, and we know that ten or twenty years down the track, that will have an effect,' she says.

With many fathers not engaged in their daughters' schooling – or at least, not to the extent of mothers – what type of father becomes over-protective of his daughter in the school environment? Experts ponder that question, because the answer is not quite as clear-cut as the effect of over-protectionism. One principal thinks long and hard before answering, 'It's dads who don't have good relation-ships with their daughters. They have some guilt over it and they just want to fix things.' I take that answer to two other principals, who between them have sixty years of experience in education. They both nod their heads in agreement. 'It's like, "I haven't been there for her, so I'll fix this,"' one says.

Let me just stick to the issue of over-protectiveness for a moment longer, because for the experts in teen growth it took up hours of discussion. They say parents are expecting schools to match the 'anxiety' and 'concerns' they hold for their daughters – and that is what is behind the strong anti-risk policies that are now in place in all-girls schools. One principal, with years of experience at a leadership level in boys' schools before moving to an all-girls school, says she was taken aback, at first, with the rigorous measures girls' schools adopted to 'protect' students. She says parents' expectations of how their sons and daughters were protected differed markedly. So what's an example? Here's one, given by a member of a school leadership team. She says that if she was leaving school, just before dusk, and saw a teenage boy waiting to be picked up, she might check what his plan was and give him a hearty goodbye wave. 'That would not happen, ever, with a girl,' she says. Her emphasis is on the word 'ever'. In that case, she'd park her car and sit with the girl until her parents had collected her, irrespective of what time that might be. She might even call them, to alert them to the fact that their daughter was waiting to be picked up. The next day, a new protocol would be developed to cover that situation. This school leader agrees that that makes good sense, but points out how different it would be with a male student, who was seen as able to fare for himself. 'That comes from parents' expectations,' she says. Schools routinely provided that extra protection for girls because parents demanded it.

Another factor operates here, and it really works against fathers wanting to engage with their daughters: while schools are keen to welcome fathers into the fold, some admit there is also a concern – which they believe is led by parents – that such a move might bring increased risks. Men, as has been reported in a previous chapter, acknowledge that they worry about this too, because of the potential to be the target of a false accusation. We've also learnt that this is partly the reason we don't have more male teachers. So isn't this an issue we need to confront? It seems soaked in irony that we are demanding fathers to be more involved in their daughters' lives and yet are treating them – certainly in some circumstances – as though they are a risk to their daughters' friends!

In considering how we parent (or indeed treat) girls and boys, care also needs to be taken to celebrate their differences. Teachers describe lunchtime at a boys' school as being typified by lots of sport, back-slapping or sitting around, but not much talking. Girls tend to be the polar opposite, chatting at a hundred kilometres an hour, talking over each other, their laughs ringing out loudly across the lunch tables. This is a point Angela White, from

Adolescent Success, makes. 'At the risk of sounding a non-feminist, boys and girls are different. They are. Physically, in brain development, socially and emotionally,' she says. 'I don't think any adolescent should be cotton-balled, and girls can do anything. Absolutely.' But White would like fathers – indeed parents in general – to approach any over-protective bent from another angle. 'If they're worried about something, then teach them the safety stuff – not do the protection thing,' she says.

Tom Matthews, who looks after guidance at St Andrew's College in Christchurch, issues this warning to fathers: treating a girl as being more vulnerable than her brother can actually lead to her becoming more vulnerable. 'It starts a belief structure in their heads,' he says. Girls, he says, can think that if they need to be protected it is because they are vulnerable. He's not alone in that view. 'Over-protective fathers are not helping their daughters develop good judgement,' one principal says. 'Being too over-protective can come at a cost,' another says. 'The girls don't learn how to deal with risks, and that's essential as they grow up.'

Dr Jennifer Mascaro, an assistant professor in family and preventative medicine at Emory University, USA, along with colleagues at Emory University and the University of Arizona, looked at how fathers interact with their daughters and their sons. This was as part of a bigger study to try to understand the factors that influence paternal caregiving. In simple terms, researchers wanted to know whether fathers interacted differently with their sons as opposed to their daughters, and whether that was related to the way their brains responded when they saw their daughters or sons. In this study, fathers were asked to wear audio-recording devices, which randomly recorded snippets of audio. Every nine minutes it came on and recorded fifty seconds of sound – but participants didn't know when it was recording and when it was not. Fathers wore the device for forty-eight hours, and the researchers coded the data based on the behaviour the fathers were engaging in, how much time they spent with their children and also the type of language they used. 'What we found was that dads with daughters were engaging in different types of behaviour more often,' said Dr Mascaro. 'They were singing and whistling a lot more often than dads with sons. They were also doing a type of interaction in which the daughter called out to the dad and the dad responded – it was called engaged responding – and that happened more often between father–daughter pairs than it did with father–son pairs.' Dr Mascaro says it is hard to determine whether the sons weren't calling out as much or whether fathers were not responding as frequently. One thing was clear, however: 'They were doing much more rough-and-tumble play – things like wrestling and tickling – than were dads with daughters.' Researchers also found difference in the language fathers were using with their daughters. Fathers of daughters used more language related to sadness, and words that related to their bodies – like 'belly', 'foot' and 'tummy'. Fathers of sons used significantly more language related to achievement – like 'win', 'top' and 'proud'.

Other studies have shown that 'rough-and-tumble' play is good for children. Indeed, a study released early in 2018 showed that parents who encouraged their children to push their limits could be protecting them from developing childhood anxiety disorders.[9] Such parenting behaviour included 'safe risk-taking', like giving a child a fright, engaging in rough-and-tumble play and letting them lose games. The research, which involved 312 families of preschoolers across Australia and the Netherlands, was conducted by Macquarie University's Centre for Emotional Health, the University of Amsterdam and the University of Reading. Dr Mascaro says rough-and-tumble play is essential for children. 'It's really good for developing emotional and social competence. I think it's potentially really important that dads of daughters aren't doing that as much. It's hard to know why that is. It could be that daughters just don't like it,' she says, 'but it could also be because of gendered ideas about how we think we should behave with sons and daughters. I know I have two little boys and we have a whole room devoted to rough-and-tumble play. It is a huge part of our lives and it makes me sad to imagine that that's not necessarily part of everyone's life, because it's such an important part of play.'

Dr Jennifer Mascaro's research was not longitudinal and did not look at child outcomes. But work that looks at that has been conducted by Dr Terry Fitzsimmons from the University of Queensland's business school. An expert on leadership, Dr Fitzsimmons has focused on gender as an issue and found, in a nutshell, that we are the sum of our experiences. 'We provide experiences for our sons that we don't provide for our daughters – for whatever reason,' Dr Fitzsimmons says. He gives the example of a parent allowing his or her son to ride his bike to a friend's place, but insisting it was not safe for a daughter to do the same. 'That creates differences, and those differences ultimately manifest themselves in the workplace. I have absolutely no doubt about that.' Dr Fitzsimmons cites that behaviour as influencing confidence-building, self-efficacy and self-reliance. He has found, in looking at leaders in the workplace, that families with both sons and daughters typically focused on their sons. Where there were all-girl families, the fathers tended to treat the daughters as 'surrogate sons', who were then taught skills their female peers might not learn – like working on vehicles, fishing, camping. He found that that exerted a positive influence on women's ability, later, to reach leadership positions. Many of our female leaders also come from hardworking, self-employed families where they learnt, from a young age, to chase their own successes. They were not handed them, and were not subjected to snow-plough parenting. 'They just had this role model of "no-one's going to give it to you – you've got to work hard for it",' he says.

So what does he believe fathers can give our daughters? 'An understanding of what it really does take to succeed in the workplace. The closer we get to gender equality, the more likely those processes will be able to be delivered by either parent, but obviously we come from a traditional background and we still haven't got there. In the majority of families, it is the father who is in the workplace.' Dr Fitzsimmons says boys are receiving lessons in confidence through unstructured activities, and girls should be provided with that same opportunity. 'Boys, as a matter of course, are allowed a high degree of freedom. In their childhood they go out and ride their bikes, go camping and do the stuff that boys do. They get up to mischief, in other words. That teaches them the boundaries of their ability; it teaches them what they can and can't do,' he says. But girls, particularly in decades past but still today to a large extent, tend to participate in more structured and highly supervised activities – like dance, drama and sport. While that gives them experience in those areas, it was not a substitute for unsupervised freedom to test their boundaries. 'The female CEOs who I interviewed were not getting that untested boundary stuff,' says Dr Fitzsimmons, 'but what they did go through

– almost all of them – was some major trauma where they had to take on an adult role. Their childhood effectively ended for a period of time, or permanently, while they took on that role as a parent or a substitute parent . . .' His take-out is that we need to challenge our daughters to provide that resilience – without the trauma or extreme hardship, of course.

And fathers can play a big part there. 'Share that knowledge that you might have picked up the hard way,' Dr Fitzsimmons says. 'Dads need to share with their daughters and their sons equally about their life experiences.'

12

Treat her well

Dr Julie Wilson Reynolds remembers her father teaching her to drive along the country roads in the Southern Highlands of New South Wales. She poses the next question: 'And you know what he did? He fell asleep while I was driving. I am a learner driver, and he's having a nap! What does that tell you?' The lesson was unequivocal. 'What I got was that he was tired and he was trusting me,' says the principal of St Hilda's on the Gold Coast. She knows that in 2018 his actions would be deemed unsafe, irresponsible even. But it was a long time ago, when so many things were different, and the message she received has stayed with her through her professional and personal life. 'The pride my dad had in me set me up for life. I have no doubt,' she says. 'My dad gave me a sense of self-belief that was extraordinary.' Girls, and particularly adolescents, she says, crave self-efficacy that can be nurtured by their fathers.

Just as a father can build a daughter's self-esteem and give her a self-belief that will help her, he can also crush it quickly – and this is central to how fathers treat their daughters. If, for example, a father demolishes an argument posed by his daughter without properly hearing it or considering it, then the subtext he delivers is this: you are not smart; you don't get it; you are immature. His daughter sees his response as a 'put-down', and the hit to her self-esteem drives a sharp wedge between father and daughter.

'Dad just says I'm wrong when I try to say what I think – so I don't bother anymore.'

'I just go quiet. I try and say something – like on refugees – and he just slaps my argument down.'

'Why bother? I'm not allowed to have an independent view. And I'm not about to agree with Dad and his views on same-sex marriage.'

All these girls are in their mid-teens. All are articulate. And all believe that expressing their genuine view would put them on a collision course with their fathers. Girls see two options here: they can antagonise their father by prosecuting their case; or they can stay quiet. The issues which divide views are often the controversial ones that dominate the news – from Australia's treatment of refugees, to its decision to legislate same-sex marriages, to whether we should become a republic. Invariably, the girls' views are supportive of change. While there were a few exceptions, most wanted refugees to have an easier path into the country, most supported same-sex marriage, and most supported the idea of a republic (although a renewed interest in the younger royals seems to mute the stridency that surfaces in the latter issue). Their fathers, on the other hand, often sat entrenched on the opposite side of those arguments. This is how the girls viewed it:

'My dad has this need to constantly be in control. If he feels as though I am making my own decisions or having my own opinion, my judgement is not valid and my decisions are almost always challenged.'

'Dad voted no (to same-sex marriage), and when he found out Australia voted yes, he got really angry. He thinks I'm wrong. How can my opinion be wrong?'

'He tries to change my mind – but he'd never change his mind.'

'Dad would just think I'm wrong and not discuss it.'

'I want to become a journalist – but Dad doesn't approve. I wish he'd give me more support and I wish he would

just acknowledge what I want to achieve in my life. My father wants to control my life, and is trying to mould me into someone I'm not.'

Those girls who saw their fathers as belittling their views were quick to tag their father as 'old' or 'old-fashioned'. 'I used to look up to my dad a lot. He was my hero,' one teen said. 'My dad is quite a lot older. He's sixty-five. There's a big age gap and I've noticed a lot of what he says is politically incorrect. It hasn't lessened how much I love him, but sometimes I look at him and think, "You really shouldn't say that."' That was at the softer end of the girls' reflections. Many used the words 'politically incorrect', but others chose 'bigot', 'out-of-date', 'racist', 'homophobic', 'misogynist' and 'rude'. And it made no difference whether their father was sixty-five or thirty-eight. It wasn't his age; it was whether girls viewed their father (and his attitude) as old. But the bigger point here was that this only came from girls who felt their fathers didn't listen to, or value, their opinion.

That doesn't surprise those teaching the girls. 'Fathers should leave being QC in the courtroom and be Dad in the lounge room,' one school leader told me. Others quickly pointed out an irony in how some fathers treat their teen daughters' opinions. These girls are being schooled to have convictions, analyse the different sides of an argument, find the supporting evidence, and then prosecute it with passion and clarity. Fathers support this, in the school context. The resurgence in the popularity of public speaking and debating shows parents want their daughters to be able to argue the veracity of a case and to stand up for themselves. They applaud strong marks for assignments based on research, analysis and communication. They like that their daughters can hold their own, in peer groups, but especially when there are boys involved. They fork out money for girls to be able to do this, well. And then the girls come home and, in many cases, their fathers – as the girls tell it – object when girls' views conflict with their fathers'.

When girls start to develop an independence from their parents, it is not only a physical and emotional separation. Sure, they no longer hold their mother's or father's hand on the way to school, and they will not feel the need to tell their parents every little detail about their day like they did when they were seven. The independence they seek is also intellectual. It's a time when they are forming their own opinions and nutting out their own ideas. 'I think some dads really struggle with that, and how they manage that can be the make or the break in their future relationship,' says Jennifer Oaten, the principal at Perth's Santa Maria College. 'When they take a risk,' Dr Julie Wilson Reynolds says, 'and say, "I actually believe X, Y and Z" – and Dad comes and demolishes that, then it is actually bigger than the argument. It's about their self-esteem and their ability to hold their own.'

Marise McConaghy from Strathcona Baptist Girls Grammar School in Melbourne, says the girls' arguments might be unsophisticated at the age of twelve, but as they progress through high school that changes, and they will want to test those arguments at home. 'They might be unwise in the ways of the world, and then they start to get into arguments with their fathers about politics, history and anything else going on,' she says. Mothers, generally, don't weigh in on those occasions as much as fathers do. But McConaghy sounds the same warning bell as her colleagues in education. A girl's father might be a surgeon, a lawyer, an accountant, a small business owner, a journalist, a captain of industry or a giant in the corporate world, but he's had decades to develop his views and finesse his arguments. He needs to remember that he is a father, at home. 'You have to go very carefully with a tender fifteen-year-old,' she says. Fathers, instead of taking offence at their daughter's viewpoint, should be proud of her attempts to show off her knowledge or test out a theory on them. Of course, some of those views might be too left-wing or too right-wing, or even plain 'wrong' to fathers. But they should not expect them to regurgitate their own views. Did we do that as teens? Of course not! Fathers should look beyond any opposition, educators say, and look for the intellectual engagement their daughter is offering. McConaghy tells fathers that it 'is about her starting to feel that she can take you on intellectually and she is trying to work out how her mind works and what her values are. She is thinking out loud to you – what a privilege! – and she trusts you to stay strong and not patronise her, but also not to annihilate her.'

That does't mean fathers need to agree with their daughters' viewpoint; just support them in developing one. 'Fathers don't need to agree with everything – quite to the contrary,' McConaghy says. 'I think it's good for the girls to be disagreed with.' Dr Julie Wilson Reynolds recommends that fathers consider how they engage in an argument. 'If they're sitting there and thinking, "That's just left field and I do not agree", take a minute and say, "I'm so excited to see you've developed some views, and how exciting that they're different to mine!"' she says. That simply acknowledges that their daughter is growing up. 'Then engage in the argument, because what they've heard is, my father's still proud of me; now we can have an argument.' Dr Wilson Reynolds says girls will read this as their father respecting them – but disagreeing with their view. Indeed, this approach might even encourage girls to come home and speak more with their fathers, because they know he will listen to them, even if he opposes their argument. 'The girls will rise to that and the dads will find that the adolescent "oh you don't know what you're talking about" or the storm-off or the sullen look dissipates.'

The take-out here is that fathers shouldn't underestimate how important it is to show their daughters respect, and to listen genuinely to their viewpoints. These two attributes are the same ones teachers demand of students when a peer is presenting their case to a class: they need to listen to what their fellow student says, and be respectful of his or her view. With that a prerequisite at schools, fathers' inability to do it at home then magnifies the issue. For their daughters, it means that they can't practise at home what they learn in the classroom, and they are less likely then to offer a view on future subjects.

This isn't easy. As principal Linda Douglas from Ruyton Girls' School says, 'We've become very good at raising gutsy girls, and they are very good at saying what they think and what they believe. Perhaps we need to be doing more in our education with girls ... to really reinforce this notion that you don't have to agree on everything with the people you love. Just because you disagree on that one thing doesn't mean that you are now mortal enemies.' Catherine O'Kane, a Brisbane principal, says it is understandable that sometimes parents can feel disappointed. 'You have this baby and then somewhere along the journey that baby becomes a young woman with her own opinions and own thoughts, and they might not be yours.' A generation ago, if our view differed from that of our parents, we might have kept it to ourself. Tamworth principal David Smith agrees, saying we should be celebrating our daughters' independent thinking and the voicing of their thoughts. 'I want kids to have their own opinions because values, in a lot of ways, are caught. You learn them as part of a process in time. I would want to encourage kids to have their own mind,' he says. It is an issue of *how* you hold that opinion. 'I don't mind if you don't have the same opinion as me, but it's how you hold that opinion,' he says. 'As an educator I want them to have an opinion, know why they have an opinion, but still respect people who are different.'

Some girls say their fathers are hell-bent on changing or 'fixing' her views, in the same way he might 'fix' the tyre on her bike. She does not want that. Indeed, she rarely wants her father to 'fix' any problem. She wants options and alternatives, and that's exactly what experts say a father should provide. Like developing a viewpoint to prosecute an argument, she wants to fashion a response to a problem by looking at the information, and determining the best answer herself. She wants her father to listen to what she says.

'There's been stuff going on at home at the moment and he wants to fix it – but he doesn't know how.'

'I don't want him to fix everything, just listen.'

'Sometimes things take time. You can't just fix things; sometimes it has to fix itself.'

'I'd like to fix it myself because I know what I want. I just want to tell him about it.'

The concept of being Mr Fix-it is alluring to dads. Many of them are practical. They want to help in a concrete, measurable way. The emotional stuff can be a bit confusing, but a problem requires a solution, and that's an easier path. Experts warn against that, however, for two reasons: first, a teen might not want to tell you something next time if you jump in to fix it too fast this time; and secondly, if you do fix it, she doesn't learn to find a solution herself. Clinical psychologist Kirrilie Smout says dads need to connect with their daughters and show they care for them, rather than solve their problems. 'Some dads find this pretty tough, because many are problem-solvers and what they want to do is to get in and fix things. Instead, fathers might say, "That sounds really tough. I'm so sorry you have to deal with that" or "Gee, that sucks". Stop, and pause, and don't say "What you should do is . . ."'

Associate Professor Michael Nagel says it is important for fathers to be good listeners . . . without necessarily offering advice. 'The girls are looking for someone to listen. You have to be a good listener. You don't have to offer solutions. More often than not, daughters aren't looking for solutions; they're looking for an ear,' he says. But he warns fathers against surrendering their leadership, particularly during the tricky teens. 'When they exercise some measure of authority it's not really a threat to their relationship; it actually brings them closer together because it shows that you care about their wellbeing and that you love them,' he says. When girls are upset, they are sometimes wondering whether they are worth the effort. 'And for dads,' says Professor Nagel, 'they have to make sure the answer is "yes". Teenagers will test their parents – sons and daughters alike.'

This doesn't translate to teen girls getting their own way, and Associate Professor Nagel gives this guide to saying 'no' to daughters. 'When you say no you are always consistent. You can't say no in one situation and agree to it in another. And the other thing is you have to be forthright and explain why you say no.' Saying no 'because it's no' doesn't cut it. Dr Briony Scott says confidence should not spill over into arrogance. 'I have no issue with young women being articulate and thoughtful and critical thinkers. I have a real issue if it then kicks over into a sense of entitlement or arrogance or being rude and dismissive,' she says. On more than one occasion, hearing a student speak rudely to their parents on a mobile phone, she has taken the phone and asked them to apologise. 'No-one gets to speak to parents rudely, ever,' she says. 'And they should be reminded every now and again of the enormous effort parents go to to help their children.'

All these suggestions revolve around listening to her. That's also the advice of Grant, one of the fathers I interviewed for this book. 'If your child takes you into their confidence, don't be the dad who thinks that he can fix everything. Most of the time you can't. But what you can do is listen to both what is said and what is left un-said.' He stresses the 'un-said', and he has learnt that through a long, painful lesson. Last year his daughter, who has just left school, wanted to see a psychologist, who urged her to talk to her parents about something she'd hidden from them for four years. At thirteen, she told her parents, she was taken into a toilet by a boy, also thirteen, and told she would be beaten up if she didn't have sex with him. She had been 'dating' him, up to this point. Retrospective vision is always clearer, and that's made it harder for Grant. 'Looking back at it, we can see there were changes in [his daughter] at the time . . . She started to lie an awful lot about silly things that were easy to check. She said she was given an extension for an assignment and then we got a note from her teacher asking where it was. It was pretty constant. We didn't actually know what was going on.' He missed the cues.

Grant now believes that the assaults happened dozens of times over a four-year period. He's a quiet father, and you can hear the anguish in his voice. 'Our family is quite well adjusted. We would have fun at the dinner table and stuff like that. Learning this was actually really hard.' The question has been on my lips for an hour. Why didn't she tell you earlier? It's obvious Grant has asked himself – and his daughter – that question too. 'She didn't know how we'd react,' he says. That will haunt him forever. His advice to others? 'Keep an open mind when it comes to your kids. Give them any chance to really tell you what is going on in their life.'

Marise McConaghy echoes this. 'Be interested in them,' she says. 'Watch TV. Talk about the issues in the news, or new movies that come out.' Lessons don't need to be embedded in each conversation. Sometimes there doesn't even need to *be* a conversation. As part of a previous research task, I talked to girls about the role they wanted their fathers to play, and one lovely answer that kept popping up was that they didn't require their fathers to talk at all! Teen girls, doing late-night assignments, love their father sitting in a chair somewhere nearby, reading. They just want to know he's there.

I was convinced of the worth of regular dates between father and daughter over and over, in researching this book. The first time it was raised was by a father on Queensland's Sunshine Coast, after I talked to parents about the challenges faced by fourteen-year-old girls. He told me that his relationship with his fourteen-year-old daughter varied each day, so he decided each weekend they would have a 'coffee date'. 'At first it was awful,' he admits. He would read the newspaper. She would play on her phone. They'd both have coffee and return home. But over time, they agreed to put the paper and the phone down and just talk. 'Now,' he told me, 'we can talk about anything.' He says he also uses that chat to show their 'commonality of values'. Another father told me that he takes his daughter to restaurants for dinner, several times a year, and even sent flowers on Valentine's Day this year. 'But why?' I asked, was their a problem? 'No,' he told me, 'but in a few years' time when boys come along, I want her to know that this is the base. He's got to shoot higher, or hopefully, she'll dump him.'

Fathers shouldn't be too concerned, either, that their daughter will be 'too cool' to be sipping an iced latte with them. These girls are thirteen, and the question was: would you like your Dad to take you on a regular date?

'Are you serious? Yes.'

'Yes! Can I pick the restaurant.'

'I'd love it because he wouldn't take my brother.'

Listening and valuing a teen's opinion, feeding her intellect, being present in her life even when she says that's not what she wants, having a good relationship with her mother, helping her to evaluate her problems, not fix them, and looking for cues where a girl's behaviour has changed noticeably are all prime skills to carry in a father's parenting kit. They require time, and patience, but story after story attest to their value. A coffee date on the way to school, or a milkshake each weekend, can make a measurable difference. Paul Dillon, author, education consultant and founder of Drug and Alcohol Research and Training Australia, says father–daughter dates have proved successful for many years. Indeed, one of the most memorable conversations he's shared with a teen followed a presentation in Canberra. A Year 10 student told him how she and her father had a 'coffee club', where they took turns to choose a venue and share a chat. 'And this young lady, completely unprovoked, told me this whole wonderful story about how much she loved her dad,' he says. That same night Paul Dillon was giving a parent talk, about the importance of connecting with your daughter. He met a man, who told him about the 'coffee club' he shared with his daughter. It was the father of the teen he had met earlier. Dillon says he explained to him how he knew that and that his daughter obviously loved him very much. 'He burst into tears,' he says.

With complex and busy lives, finding that time for a date is not always easy. But daughters will know that this is time Dad wants to spend only with her. And daughters will remember it. Take this comment, from a seventeen-year-old. 'I think most fathers find female teenagers very complex and I very much agree that we are,' she says. 'My father struggled to relate to me and to understand any problems I was facing and it became frustrating so I think he gave up and stopped making the effort. I struggled with that lack of understanding a lot in my early teenage years because it's so important to have that relationship with your dad and I found it really hard to hear, see or discuss someone's bond with their dad because mine wasn't there.'

13

Boyfriends, online and off

Detective Inspector Jon Rouse, the head of Australia's Task Force Argos, is worried about thousands of young girls, but one particular child springs to mind on this day. She's only young, perhaps six or seven, he estimates, and she's in her bedroom somewhere. It's what she's doing that's brought her to his attention. On an iPad or some other mobile device, she's filming herself and putting on a show that strikes a discord with her young years. 'It's horrific,' Inspector Rouse says. 'She puts on a show that's quite disturbing – and that's putting it at a minimum.' This find – of a girl acting precociously, sexually – is not new to Inspector Rouse or his investigators. 'We see quite young kids – from six, seven, eight and nine – getting online and producing material.' The internet has no boundaries, and that makes his investigation much harder. The child could be in Sydney or Melbourne or Hobart. She could also be in Paris or Seattle or London. But wherever she is, her video has the potential to spread like wildfire, into the wrong hands. Locating her is like finding a needle in a haystack. Inspector Rouse's team of investigators will start by looking at the images to find anything recognisable. It's painstakingly slow; disproportionate with the speed the images travel. They will look at the room's background. Does that hold a clue? A calendar? An open window that might hint at the season? Floorboards that are more likely to be manufactured in one country than another? Sometimes the little girl is found. Other times she's not.

Our daughters are growing up in a raunch culture – a culture which promotes overtly sexual representations of women. The pressure to conform is extraordinary. The influence of marketing messages, built on billion-dollar budgets, hones in on teen girls trying to find their identity. This is unfair at a time when their critical thinking skills are still developing and the power of the peer group is at its peak. 'Why can't I share?' 'All my friends get a Brazilian wax and they're only twelve!' 'Everyone is wearing these bikinis!' 'I'm not doing something wrong posting it on Instagram – it's someone else's fault if they send it to everyone else.' 'By the way, how many "likes" have I got on that post?' The point here is that girls are growing up in an acutely sexual culture that saturates their lives. From friends' posts to billboards, television shows to schoolyard dramas, the message is the same: this is what's in, and if you don't conform, you'll soon be out! Where once pornography had to be actively sought, and was difficult for kids to access, it is now just a click away, and in many cases it's an accidental click at that.

Dr Tim Hawkes is the author of of several books, including *Ten Conversations You Must Have with Your Son* and *Ten Leadership Lessons You Must Teach Your Teenager*. He says the 'birds and the bees' talk that sixty years ago might have been given to girls at the age of sixteen, now needs to be delivered to girls nearer the age of twelve. 'Girls are maturing at an ever-younger age. They are also being reared in a culture where porn is endemic even among "tweenagers",' he says. Police and educators agree. Often, police will be called to talk to boys who believe that what they see online is what their new girlfriend wants, but is too shy to request. Often, too, the teen girl might assent to something she doesn't really want to do because she believes her peers are doing the same, and she doesn't want to stand out. Educators say that premature sexualisation of girls is a significant contributor to depression. 'They're not allowed to be girls,' Dr Hawkes says. 'We are buying bras for babies! Even when it comes to relationships . . . what's happening is they think they have to be able to do all the tricks of a seasoned porn star. No wonder there is this anxiety, particularly amongst girls.'

Tim Hawkes' words are strong and direct, but no-one contradicts them. While evidence suggests our children are not having sex any younger than they might have twenty years ago, they are going 'around sex', one Year 9 teacher says. What does that mean? It means that oral sex now is part of a teenager's sexual repertory, because in the minds of teens it is not *really* defined as sex. It means that anal sex now falls into the same category too. This doesn't mean your mid-teen daughter, or her friends, are engaging in these activities, but girls in their cohort may be, and chances are they are talking about it. Rainbow parties, considered a myth by some, do happen and were raised twice during this project: once by a principal and another time by teenagers. (For those who are new to this term, it is where girls, wearing lipstick, take turns in fellating males in sequence, leaving a rainbow of colours on their penises.)

Many other sexual activities have also become part of the teenage scene, a number of them based around activities popular on porn sites. 'Kids are learning about sex from pornographic sites and they think that's what you have to do,' Inspector Jon Rouse says. 'A lot of pornography is brutal, demeaning and degrading. It's not consistent with what loving consensual parents do, or partners do.' And that, he says, needs to be addressed – starting with parents, at home. 'You'd have to be naive to think your kids haven't seen something. You really would,' he says. Maree Crabbe, director of Reality & Risk: Pornography, Young People and Sexuality, is being asked more and more by schools for help on the issue, which she says is affecting young women. She urges parents to have conversations with their daughters around what they might see. 'A lot of dads long for their daughters to be treated with respect and to feel happy and safe. We can't just assume that is going to happen. We need to have those conversations,' she says.

Warnings about taking half-naked selfies, or the determination to have the most 'likes' on Instagram, or distributing inappropriate material, are also so common that you have to wonder if the message about the dangers involved has been muted. Certainly all of those behaviours are on the rise. 'Kids are just doing it without any concept of the consequences,' Inspector Rouse says. He says a type of 'sextortion' is also becoming far too common. This can be where a young girl will expose herself, take a photo or movie, and send it to someone. That recipient will then capture it, save it, and later demand the child does more. If they refuse, they will threaten to make it public in some way. Fear of getting caught, or having their parents find out, can influence children's compliance. 'Kids aren't equipped with how to deal with that, so in many cases they will comply,' Inspector Rouse says. He says that education has to start with parents at home, and many of them were shirking that responsibility. 'They're completely naive to all these things that are going on. Honestly, if I had an eight- or nine-year-old kid now, all mobile devices would be taken off them before they went to bed and the wi-fi turned off. That would be a house rule.' He knows it's harder than it used to be for busy parents to police. 'When I started, it was easy. You had a big PC monitor in the lounge or the bedroom. Now it's "night Mum, night Dad" and then they're in bed and under the covers with an iPad or something else.'

Other books have looked at internet controls and girls' use of social media. Here, I'm aiming to explain to fathers how they might play a positive role in how their daughters see themselves and who they choose as a partner. The girls' online world is pivotal to that – and fathers are absolutely vital, here. Indeed, Hertfordshire University researchers last year found positive, supportive schools and family communication, particularly with fathers, was protective against online bullying.[10] Other research shows that a girl's relationship with her father moulds her views on what to expect – and indeed what to accept – once she is looking to form a partnership. 'In my years of psychology practice,' Dr Jennifer Kromberg writes in *Psychology Today*, 'I've met very few women who did not unconsciously or consciously pick a romantic partner based on the characteristics of her father.' The girls support that, too. Sandie says: 'I find that as I get older and I'm getting into relationships I look for a guy with qualities and traits my Dad has,' she says. Dr Kromberg points out that she doesn't mean physical characteristics – although that might be part of it. 'I mean relational pattern characteristics,' she says. 'Even the women who state they chose partners who were opposite of their dad are basing their decisions on the relationship (or non-relationship) with Dad.'[11] Those comments are backed up repeatedly, with experts pointing to the flip side where an unhealthy father–daughter relationship exists. Sometimes, if a girl can't find acceptance at home, she might go looking for it elsewhere, *and* earlier than she should.

Author and father–daughter expert Linda Nielsen in 'How Dads Affect Their Daughters into Adulthood' poses the question of how a father influences his daughter's romantic life – who she dates, when she starts having sex, and the quality of her relationships with men. She provides a widely endorsed answer. 'Not surprisingly, a girl who has a secure, supportive, communicative relationship with her father is less likely to get pregnant as a teenager and less likely to become sexually active in her early teens. This, in turn, leads to waiting longer to get married and to have children – largely because she is focused on achieving her educational goals first.'[12] Professor Nielsen says that a well-fathered daughter is also more likely to have relationships with men who are 'emotionally intimate and fulfilling', and these women (as they become) generally have more satisfying and longer-lasting marriages. 'During the college years, these daughters are more likely than poorly fathered women to turn to their boyfriends for emotional comfort and support and they are less likely to be "talked into" having sex. What is surprising is not that fathers have such an impact on their daughters' relationships with men, but that they generally have more impact than mothers do.'

This last point shouldn't be lost when we are talking about the towering influence fathers can have on their daughters' romantic lives – and those fathers' confusion about what to do. 'How do I handle boyfriends?' one father asked. 'How do dads become a person who can talk about boys (good and bad) without seeming like we are preaching, being totally unrealistic or chauvinistic?' another said.

This is what teen girls are saying about their fathers and potential boyfriends.

'In my experience, which granted isn't very much, girls don't want to talk to their fathers about boys or sex . . . ever . . . it's just too awkward. So, when a boy is talked about, they are usually a potential long-termer, aka a boyfriend for longer than two weeks.'

'Dad says he'll have the shotgun out when I get boyfriends. Like he doesn't even have one. It's not even

funny, and he wouldn't say that to my brothers! Like, "When you bring a girlfriend home I'll get a shotgun." He'd never say that.'

'When we have a bad break-up with a boy (which is pretty much all break-ups) we want our dads to give us a hug, tell us we're beautiful and then never ever talk about it again.'

Girls are just as at sea as their fathers and wanted to know how to handle these situations.

'Can you cover boyfriends, please? Dad would be a bit agitated about that. Can you tell him to chill?'

'Can you do something on stereotypes? I reckon it would be strange asking Dad, not my mum, about boys. It would be like weird.'

'Can you give Dad some tips on how to handle it when I get a boyfriend?'

Before we get to the 'dos', let's just address a couple of 'dont's' for dads. Don't lie. 'My dad won't tell me when he had his first girlfriend or anything like that. He just lies about all that. He says he had his first girlfriend when he was thirty,' Chloe says. Don't follow the lead of this girl's dad. 'When your daughter says "OMG, I'm so fat" DON'T reply, as my dad does, by saying "Yes you are looking a little big", but say something along the lines of basically "No, you're not, you're perfect as you are",' Tamara, seventeen, says. Don't put yourself in competition for your daughter's attention. 'My dad was very surprisingly accepting of a boy. He just got upset that I stopped spending time with him!' And don't befriend a daughter's new boyfriend. This happens more than you might imagine. Fathers inviting their daughter's boyfriend to the football on a Friday night. Or fishing with a group of blokes on the weekend. Working on a car together in the backyard. Monopolising his visits to the family home to talk rugby. Psychologist and author Andrew Fuller says it is not uncommon, and he knows some fathers who have secretly stayed friends with their daughter's boyfriend once the couple had parted. 'So many men, because they don't invest in their own friendship world, are vulnerable to this,' he says. They might not have made new friends as they've grown older, and their 'friendship intelligence' reflects the time when they were a teenager. 'So a logical companion is their daughter's partner.' It's not advisable. 'That would be creepy,' one fourteen-year-old responds, when asked. To her it would be akin to her mother calling her girlfriend and making a shopping date. 'They're like a different generation. Why would dads want to do that anyway?' Another says this: 'What then happens when you break up? Does that mean your dad might take your boyfriend's side?'

Andrew Fuller also points to a girl's relationship with her mother to emphasise the importance of fathers, once girls mature to romantic interests. This area is worth a thesis of its own, but it could be the competition that sometimes exists between mothers and daughters, or the disapproval society carries of women who appear sexy in public, or the natural push by girls away from their mothers – but in so many cases daughters might turn to their father for acceptance of their boyfriend. It's a tricky place, but three simple rules experts provided along the way include: first, show your daughter the treatment she should expect in a relationship, secondly, keep the lines of communication through this period open and be interested in what she tells you; and thirdly, a boyfriend is a daughter's companion, not a father's friend.

If teen girls won't broach the subject of boys, that doesn't mean fathers can't. 'I told Mum first,' Eliza says. 'But once I did talk to Dad he was quite supportive. I wondered where it was coming from. But that made me open up more about other stuff to him.' Mothers tend to be more encouraging. 'My mum's actually very supportive of relationships. She's like, "Emma, go get yourself a boyfriend. Have some fun while you are still young." I've started to get some friends who are boys and Dad just laughs at me. Dad doesn't have a lot of interest but Mum's pushing me.' Sophia is the same. 'My mum would be happy for me but my dad would definitely be intimidating to the boy. He's told me a hundred times I can't have a boyfriend until I'm thirty.' And that is still fourteen years away.

So, accepting fathers have a crucial role here, what can they do? As outlined earlier, girls learn from the behaviour their fathers model. That means fathers can show daughters, through their own treatment of women, including the girls' mother, the respect that should colour a relationship. School principal Linda Douglas says girls learn from the specific interactions they see – how their father engages with their mother, the relationship between their father and sister, and their father and themselves. Angela White from Adolescent Success says the father's influence is so strong because it is the girl's first male relationship. 'That's the model she's had. For most thirteen-year-old girls that might be the only model they will have had. So fathers are teaching their daughters how to relate to men without realising.' Deputy principal Julie Feeney says girls also need to understand 'how the other half of the gender operates'. 'The way he treats her mother is a great reflection for the girl to understand what a positive heterosexual relationship is,' she says. By the same token, negative relationships can be role-modelled. One principal says his experience is that 'Mum and Dad openly squabbling' has an impact on girls, especially in Year 10. That was because it was the age when they were more aware of how relationships operated and understood the role gender played. 'Some of those kids really crave attention, and the risk is they'll crave it from someone else, without thinking carefully about it,' he says. 'That's what scares me.'

Kirrilie Smout says fathers will have a perspective on relationships that mothers might not have, and needed to ask questions of their daughters. Indeed, she says, ask ten questions before offering any piece of advice. 'Tell me what you think of this guy?' 'How do you manage that?' 'Why do you think he does that?' Smout continues, 'If you have that conversation and then say "You know what I think?", you get to shape how girls think about their relationships with boys. That's a gift.' Fathers should also be reminded that a daughter's problems are not his to *solve*. 'It is her journey and you are not responsible for making sure she never gets hurt. You can't do that and it's not your job,' she tells fathers.

Paul Dillon has sympathy for fathers here, saying that seeing a daughter become a young woman can be difficult. 'They remember when they were young men and what they did with young women. They don't want to see their daughters in that kind of light. The connection between fathers and daughters is unique and special and it's something you can't quite explain,' he says. Parents flip from a management role to a consulting role when their girls are in their teens, and the relationship changes. 'If you can find a way of keeping connected during that time, adolescence is going to be so much better,' Paul Dillon says.

David Smith from Calrossy Anglican School, Tamworth, says girls benefit from having a wide circle of friends – of both sexes – early on, including some not tied to their school. 'We encouraged our girls to have lots and lots of healthy friendships – through sport, through church, through all sorts of different things,' he says. Alana, fifteen, says her father approaches it in the same way. 'I was at a co-ed school and am now at an all-girls school. Dad says it's really, really important to have friends who are boys.' Single-gender schools can struggle with this. In writing *Being 14*, it stood out to me that teen girls at single-gender schools spend far too much time talking about boys. At the co-ed schools, it was more matter-of-fact. Boys were peers, or science partners. Asking someone to your semi-formal was akin to asking a friend. That means, in single-gender schools, girls have to be given the means of meeting boys and developing wide friendships, particularly if they don't have brothers. While extracurricular activities allow that, some schools are also embarking on joint high-school classes or activities to facilitate that.

New Zealand guidance educator Tom Matthews says 'keeping the conversation open' heads his list for fathers confronted with their daughter's first boyfriend. 'A father's role is to stay in a dialogue so they can maintain influence, and pulling the shotgun line out is a fake control. What we should be doing is saying, let's talk about this . . .' The consequences are obvious, he says, if fathers choose not to do that. If a girl feels as though she can't raise the subject with her father, she won't. That means she will be making decisions without his input. Angela White adds something else here. She warns against shutting down any conversation on boys because it can hinder the relationship when daughters push boundaries and shatter fathers' expectations. 'If they don't act in the way you expect, there has to be a way for them to recover from that. If you say you have to be in by 9:30 pm and they don't get in until ten, there's a consequence for that – but there has to be a way to safely recover without it being the end of the world,' she says. This is a skill, requiring flexibility, which fathers may not have needed earlier in a daughter's life. 'And the reason it's required is that a purpose of adolescence is to push boundaries.' If a girl breaks a rule – like, once again, arriving home after a 9:30 pm curfew – her father should explain why he was worried, and provide a consequence. But don't, she says, allow it to become 'a make or break issue' where it's hard to retrieve the situation.

Rules are important, says Beth Oakley, deputy principal at Wenona. 'This precious little pure innocent thing has become a woman before his eyes and he knows how other guys see her and is protective about that. I think that is so hard,' she says. 'I think it's good that dads want to meet the guy. Girls think that is weird. But if he is relaxed about that and doesn't bring out the checklist and have an interview first . . . he should do that. He needs to say that to his daughter.' Other rules might be similar to those enacted when teen girls go to a party. 'He's not going to beep the horn out the front; he's going to come to the front door. And here's the curfew time,' she says. Girls mature at different ages, and in some instances twelve-year-olds are going to the movies with boys, just as there are eighteen-year-olds who do not have a boyfriend. 'I always say, be the parent who picks up,' Beth Oakley says. 'If the boundaries and expectations have been in place from a young age, it's not a surprise at an older age – you just let the rope out a little bit more and more each year . . .'

Tim Hawkes appeals to fathers to be honest, too. 'An honest sharing of the likelihood of falling in love more than once is something that a father can talk about. Also important is for a father – often seen as the disciplinarian – to give a guarantee of love and acceptance whatever happens in terms of sexual orientation, sexual escapades and sexual mistakes.' Many teen girls still fear revealing their sexual orientation to parents. 'I'm wondering whether I should put it in a letter,' one girl tells me. Beth Oakley has some advice for fathers in these circumstances. 'Say to her, "It doesn't change who you are, it doesn't change how I feel about you, but I need to be honest because I'm struggling at this stage because I've got this vision of my future where I have grandchildren and I have a son-in-law. That's the stumbling block for me, darling. The stumbling block is not you, and my love for you hasn't changed a bit. It's my dreams and the things I had foreseen that I have to re-imagine and re-picture, and that will just take some time to process."'

Dr Hawkes says he likes to think good fathers act as a 'strong island from which children take their bearings'. 'The fastest growing ailment among young people is depression. The instances of depression, of poor self-worth, of people being referred to medical experts because of psycho-social problems, has grown exponentially,' he says. 'Much of this relates to the fact that we don't have those firm islands; there's an insecurity in that.' That's made worse by girls having to make decisions in a highly sexualised culture, where pornography is easily accessible and individual freedoms mean we accept behaviour we should not. 'I think it's a pretty sad indictment on our society,' he says. 'One of the biggest victims of all of this is our daughters.'

14

Provider or parent

'I really feel like I mucked it up with her and it's my fault,' one father wrote to me. 'I have always done everything financially with her – schools, braces on teeth – but emotionally I missed the mark with her big time. Makes me very sad, to be honest, as I feel I failed her – but I guess time will tell.' He says his daughter is a 'great kid and I love her to death'. 'But to be honest I have tried and tried and virtually given up. I keep telling myself it may take years but she will eventually come around and let me in,' he writes. 'Out of all the things I have on my mind with jobs, money, relationships with others and day-to-day life, this is my biggest concern and plays on my mind the most.'

This father has been doing what he believes is right: providing for his family, ensuring his daughter attends a good school, spending thousands of dollars on her teeth, setting her up for the future by giving her a good start. But it's the return on his investment – the relationship he now has with his daughter – that is bedevilling him. He is not alone; that same sentiment is mirrored by other fathers who have worked hard to provide security for their families. Some lament the long hours at the office and the days spent away from home. They were not sunning themselves in the Bahamas or putting the family's fortunes on number seven at a casino in Las Vegas; they were working to ensure their families had a comfortable house, annual holidays and a savings kitty. But has it been worth it? Has their role as chief money provider impoverished their role at home? 'Don't get me wrong,' Julie, sixteen, says. 'We have everything, including a huge house. But that doesn't mean I get to see my dad.' Or this answer from Mary: 'My dad always says, "You never appreciate me. I've given so much to you and you don't appreciate it." I appreciate my dad so much – it really hurts when he says that kind of thing. He had a pretty rough life. He moved away from home when he was fifteen and moved to Australia. He's paid for my granny's life. He was the breadwinner of his family and our family. He feels as though he's put in so much and he hasn't got it back.'

Do fathers see themselves as providers or parents? And, by focusing on one, does it follow that there will be less time, and expertise, to focus on the other? Certainly work done by the Australian Institute of Family Studies shows that long working hours and schedules that are not family-friendly have an impact on the time a parent spends with their children. In one study, 'Long hours and Longings', which was conducted in 2017, more than one-third of children believed their father worked too much. 'Children's voices are rarely heard in debates about work and family, yet they can be discerning observers of how their father's job impacts the family,' researchers found. 'They appear to be aware of the importance of those jobs for family income, but also of the impact of those jobs on family time.' Children were also more likely to say their father worked too much if he worked outside of standard daytime hours. 'This was especially so if Dad worked nights, evenings or rotating shifts,' they found. 'If Dad worked some weekends, children were also more likely to say he worked too much.'[13]

Traditionally, fathers have been employed in full-time paid work, while mothers have worked part-time or not in paid employment. But mothers also spend more time than fathers doing the household work – and that includes both child care and domestic work. The Australian Institute of Family Studies (AIFS) pooled data from the Household, Income and Labour Dynamics in Australia (HILDA) survey and found that it was uncommon for child-care activities to be done always or usually by fathers. This was the case across the board – from ensuring that children were dressed, to staying with ill children, ferrying them to and from places, getting them to bed and helping with their homework. It was only in stay-at-home father families that it was more likely these tasks were done always or usually by the father. (Australia has about 75 000 stay-at-home father families, which represents about 4 per cent of two-parent families. This has changed little over the past five years, and compares to almost 500 000 families with stay-at-home mothers. According to the AIFS, stay-at-home mother families are 'considerably more likely' to have younger children compared to stay-at-home father families.) The AIFS says that while stay-at-home dads took on more responsibility for child care than fathers in other families, the 'average stay-at-home dad is still far from "Mr Mum"'.[14]

Anecdotally, at least, it makes sense that the parent who is most often home is the parent who has the ear of their children. They are more likely to be present when their child arrives home, or more likely to pick them up when school calls to say they are ill. They are also more likely to cook dinner, pack the lunches and pull the lunch box out of a school bag.

'It was more Dad working, and then Mum got the more dominant job so now Dad is the person who does everything. He works from home as well. Because Dad

picks me up, I tell him things first and then probably tell Mum later. It's because he's there.'

'My mum does everything. She stopped working when she had kids. She picks me up, does all the cooking and cleaning, makes my lunches and sometimes I don't see my dad for days. If I have a problem I go straight to Mum. Mum even goes to all the parent teacher interviews. I don't think Dad has ever been to one. He doesn't even go to speech night for me.'

'Dad sees his role as more of the provider and Mum as the parent.'

While in the first example, it was the girl's father who was 'there', it is still far more likely in 2018 for mothers to be the primary caregivers. But here's the pinch. Even when mothers are in the workforce, they still pick up most of the jobs at home. Dr Jennifer Baxter, senior research fellow at the AIFS, says that even when mothers work full-time and young children are involved, they tend to do more of the child care and domestic work. She says it has to be remembered, though, that fathers in full-time employment often work longer hours than mothers employed full-time. Social researcher Mark McCrindle says that men have both increased their participation in unpaid domestic work over the past two decades and the time spent each week in child rearing. 'But the gap between their contribution and that of their female partner is still quite big,' he says. 'They haven't come close to closing that gap.' He says this trend has played out as women's participation in the paid workforce has increased. Author, academic and researcher Dr Stephen Holden says unpaid household work is equivalent to about 50 per cent of GDP. 'Who does this work? Women do,' he says, at a rate of almost two times that of men – and that's even greater if there are children. However, he says that while women do about two-thirds of the unpaid household work, men do about two-thirds of the paid work, and that those ratios had not changed much over the past decade.

None of this means that fathers aren't trying to up their workload at home. Girls repeatedly offer examples – without being prompted – of their fathers trying to make a splash in the house, either by cooking dinner or taking up the primary-caregiver role on a weekend. Lovely examples surfaced, of fathers encouraging their children to allow their mothers to sleep in each Saturday, or whisking their mother out to breakfast and organising the children to clean the house and make lunch as a surprise.

'My dad is in the defence force. He works longish hours but tries to be involved as much as he can. He makes the lunches and drives us to afternoon sports, but Mum is dominant in the household chore area.'

'He's full-on on the weekends he's home, but mainly taking my brothers to sport. So while he tries, it doesn't mean I spend more time with him.'

New South Wales Principal David Smith has three adult daughters and doesn't doubt we are still locked into stereotypes. 'Mum brings up the kids and Dad works, and where Mum works as well, she's still expected to take on that role.' He said schools needed to play a role in modelling behaviour, educating parents and encouraging men to step forward. He tells the story of a Sydney seminar he attended where a lead educator told the audience that his job was to teach boys to be good men, good husbands and good fathers. 'And the principal of one of the girls' schools was there and she said, "If I actually said we were trying to help our girls to be good mothers and good wives, I'd be shot. We are equipping our women to be high powered, competent and capable – to be anything they want."'

But are we putting the same effort into ensuring men aren't butting up against a glass ceiling when it comes to parenting? Certainly mothers also play the greater parent volunteer role inside the school grounds. These responses are all taken from members of school leadership teams; each is from a different State.

'A lot of the schooling side of things is looked after by the mothers, and the fathers seem to have little actual

time – in terms of minutes – where they interact with their daughters – to the point where you say, "What year is your daughter in?" and they say, "Year 10? Or Year 9?"'

'I don't see much involvement from dads at school, and that hasn't changed in my twenty years. You see it at primary school: sometimes they drop them off; they might attend Father's Day breakfast. But it is mums we see more. In senior school, we don't see dads much at all.'

'As far as I can see, parenting in the schools context is outsourced to the mothers.'

'I don't know how it plays out at home, but fathers are largely absent from schools – and when we say to the girls, "Who is your biggest role model?" it's always Mum.'

Although fathers' involvement is dwarfed by mothers', many schools are seeing fathers wanting to engage more.

'I'm seeing in my school community that you don't have to be female to be feminist,' one principal said.

'I think we're certainly seeing fathers who are not always the traditional breadwinner of the family, we're seeing fathers who are organising their workdays so they can be at school functions whereas previously it was "the father can't make those times". I'm increasingly seeing fathers making sure that they are present at junior school

assembly, just like the working women are getting to the junior assembly.'

'It's from a low base, but I am trying to structurally find a way to include more fathers. They want to get involved and they are not looking for board positions or to be the King Pooh-Bah. They just want to do stuff.'

That trip from provider to parent is a logical one. Certainly, in many households the provider role has been diminishing as women increase their paid workforce participation. Men are no longer compelled in some instances to work the same hours if their partner has picked up work also. In some cases this has also been driven by families wanting fathers to engage more with their children, during school hours. And that's set to continue, Mark McCrindle says. 'For this next generation, if the norm continues and income does follow the education levels, then we will have women out-earning men,' he says. 'That means the provider role, in terms of who's got the stable job, who's got the growing career, who's got the earning potential, is shifting.'

While different schools experience different levels of engagement by fathers, two things are crystal clear. First, it is coming from a low base, so that even in those schools where fathers' involvement is growing, it remains secondary to that of mothers. The second point is the uniformity of opinion on the value of having fathers embrace the parenting role and not refer to themselves as 'the provider'. Their daughters will embrace that, arguing that fathers sometimes bring a 'chill' factor.

'I've gone to Mum several times and said something as simple as, "This teacher is so irritating" and she's like, "Right, I'll report it to the school". She wants to take everything up with the school and I just want to tell someone what is going on. Whereas my dad will give me advice but he'll understand that you might just want to talk about it. You might just want someone to understand, so I feel more comfortable talking to Dad about that.'

'My mum says, "I need to talk to the school", "I need to call this person's mother and this person's mother" and Dad's just, "Love, screw all of them."'

'I talk Mum out of it most of the time – but she's ready to run up to the principal's office and complain on my behalf any time. Sometimes I just don't tell her because I'm worried. But if it's really huge, Dad will write an email – and then Mum will have to edit it!'

One principal puts it this way. 'Dads to me seem to be much more grounded and to roll with the punches. My sense is that if we saw dads more involved then perhaps we would get less of the preciousness around how girls are treated and perhaps we wouldn't get as much of that overdramatisation of the small, which mums sometimes do.' Another principal says he believes that mothers often become too emotionally invested in advocating for their daughters. He gives the example of a friendship fallout among teenage girls. 'Women almost feel the pain of their daughter. Fathers will just say, "Make new friends in the class."'

Schools see a role for themselves in structuring an environment in which fathers can be more engaged. This has become evident in recent years where a surge in school social events has put the focus on fathers – from Father's Day breakfasts to father–daughter dances, to dads-only tuckshop duty. Some of these events have been influenced by the challenge fathers face in finding meaningful ways to interact with their daughters through those teenage years, when they are increasingly spending time and being influenced by their peers. Several schools this year opened – and marketed – their International Women's Day events to fathers for the first time. 'In all of our events, it's that consciousness that fathers should be part of this too,' one school leader says.

So if fathers genuinely want to be more involved, and we know their daughters would benefit greatly as a result of that, why don't they? A myriad of answers flow. 'I can sense something different going on where fathers are trying to get in, but women have to let them in too,' one principal says. The crucial role mothers can play here – including in standing back and allowing their partners in – is examined in the next chapter, but a host of other reasons pop up too. Systemically, perhaps, the current environment works against men. The first time I heard this, I considered it a cop-out by fathers. But, after talking to so many of them, it is obvious that overzealous school protection policies, unfriendly workplaces and even a communal suspicion of men makes it hard on many to take that step forward. Women are more able – and in many cases welcome – to volunteer in the classroom or take up tuckshop duties or wander the school grounds unaccompanied. Schools admit this, and they mirror the same refrain. The impetus for the protectionist policies in schools comes from parental expectation; the schools are simply responding to what parents are demanding. Fathers are also often shut out of those volunteer school positions because of family-unfriendly workplaces. While strides forward have been made in the last decade, those breadwinners who want to balance work and family life still find it difficult because of workplace and government policies. At work, men are seen as workers, not necessarily fathers, whereas women are often considered to be both.

Dr Stephen Holden says separation – especially where a mother gains majority custody of the children – can also make it difficult for men who want to transfer from provider to parent. In this situation, a father's involvement can kindle undeserved suspicion, and men are acutely aware of that. He gives the example of a father shopping for his daughter's underwear: he is deemed a security risk. A single father, searching for an au pair online, becomes the target of suspicion. Dr Holden says he knows the latter from personal experience when after his marriage ended he went looking for help with his son. Despite advertising for au pairs, he never received any responses, so he called the agency responsible for placements. 'But you're a single dad,' he was told, 'and they're all girls.' A couple of weeks later, though, he was sent an applicant who fitted the bill. 'They had great child-care experience, nieces and nephews,' he says, before pausing. 'And it was a guy.' Stephen Holden is honest here. He says he then thought, 'Am I sure I want a male looking after my young child? And then I thought, I'm just doing exactly the same as everybody else!' The male au pair was employed and became a valuable addition to his family. 'But I had to overcome my own prejudice,' he admits. He gives a second example of finding a toddler one afternoon, on the beach. He asked her where her parents were. 'Then this woman flew out of left field and came at me screaming and shouting,' he says. Dr Holden says he was annoyed and hurt by the incident. As a father, he understood how quickly children can escape from their parents. 'But I do think it's wrong thinking I'm the enemy.'

The stranglehold of suspicion is felt by many men. During interviews for this book, some fathers said they hadn't confronted it, others said they ignored it, but many said it changed how they dealt with their daughter, her friends, and teenage girls in general. Inspector Jon Rouse from Task Force Argos calls it a 'sad indictment on our society'. My interview with him occurred shortly after a public discussion had arisen on the subject of whether it was appropriate for a father to bathe with his baby daughter. 'A knee-jerk reaction!' he said. 'I remember having showers with my little girl. For God's sake, that doesn't make me a child sex offender! If I'm walking around a pool and taking pictures of lots of kids, that's really suspicious and inappropriate,' he says. 'But if my little girl is jumping into the pool and I take a picture, I've got a right to do that.' Inspector Rouse urges fathers to ignore the suppositions of others, in the same way we still take holidays or visit city centres despite the few isolated terror attacks that have happened in these places.

All this means is that for fathers to become more engaged, the community needs to change – families, schools and workplaces. Tim Hawkes says schools need to focus on becoming more 'parent-friendly'. 'There's still the sense that there's a de-militarised zone at the front gate of some schools, where the idea is that you park your student and then you disappear, and we'll do the job of educating for you,' he says. But it also requires change by fathers. They cannot afford to take a step back as their daughters climb through adolescence. 'Dads need to be careful that they do not spend so much time trying to be someone outside of the home that they forget to be someone within it,' Dr Hawkes says. Innately wired to provide, he says, sometimes fathers choose the sacrificial approach – 'Of course I love you, I pay for your school fees, don't I?' Or they become the 'blue pencil dad, the editing dad, the just-wait-till-your-father-gets-home dad, the dad that deals with the heavy stuff'.

Despite the difficulties, dads *are* advancing into new parenting territory. Wenona's Beth Oakley says greater engagement by fathers reflects a generational change. This is evident in the number of daughters now having their fathers present at the birth of their babies, or fathers who are comfortable showing emotion and hugging their friends. 'I am hoping that there is a climate where it's okay to seek professional help from a counsellor,' she says. 'Anecdotal evidence around that is that dads are saying that they went and got help ... whereas ten years ago a father would never reveal that. I have several dads saying, "I'm getting support through this" and "I'm working through this". That's fantastic.' These moves, instigated by fathers who want to be more engaged in their daughters' lives, fly in the face of a default position you see in other cases, where fathers believe 'the kids are fine because my wife is here and it's being managed'. Parenting expert Maggie Dent says that up until recently fathers told her how they struggled with the social norms around fathering 'because they were the soft man who wanted to be more in their children's lives' but believed it was easier said than done. 'Dads now are loving the fact that it's completely acceptable for them to be the stay-at-home dad, the hands-on parent, going into the Kindy and watching their child.' The hurdle now is the lack of knowledge they have to draw on – because their own fathers had not been 'hands on'. 'They don't want to know about the research,' Dent says. 'They want to know what to do.'

Professor Gayle Kaufman, the author of *Superdads: How Fathers Balance Work and Family in the 21st Century*, classifies three types of fathers – Old Dads who look after their family through paid employment, New Dads who see themselves as providers and involved parents, and Super Dads who see themselves as fathers first and everything else (including work) second. 'What distinguishes the super dads is how they respond . . . what they do in terms of their work life and if they make adjustments to their work life because of their role as father,' says Professor Kaufman. Those who made that decision didn't regret it.

But where does that leave mothers? And what is the role of mothers when a father – even belatedly – wants to step up and try his hand at being a more engaged parent?

15

A mum's role

Maggie Dent puts it this way: 'There are two ways of changing a nappy and both ways are valid.' Her message is that mothers need to allow fathers to parent too. A father's methods might not mirror a mother's, but that doesn't matter. Wenona principal Dr Briony Scott describes it a bit like stacking the dishwasher. You might do it, over and over again, before complaining that 'I'm always the one stacking the dishwasher'. 'Then someone else stacks it and you then go and restack it because they haven't stacked it in the way you have – and you just have to back off a little bit.' Who hasn't experienced that? Who hasn't played the martyr? It's a safe place to be. 'I know because I've played it myself,' Dr Scott says. '"You don't understand how tough it is for me. I work, I raise the family. I do the lunches." There's an element of truth in the sense that somebody is usually managing the family and is the dominant player. But it is easy then to get protective of that because you are the central player.'

Any mother, or even male primary caregivers, will recognise similar examples. Father arrives home after work on Friday night saying, 'Let's go camping, kids!' Mother might have already planned something for Saturday afternoon. It will mean missing a ballet lesson or a cricket game at the beginning of the season. So the camping trip is outlawed. He should have asked earlier. It's not his right to walk in and up-end plans. Or it might be an 8 pm swim in the family pool. He's just arrived home from work and the children are almost ready for bed. He tells them to get their swimming costumes on. Mother knows this means a late bedtime and tired children in the morning. That will make it harder tomorrow afternoon, when their father is safely at work and not around to deal with it. Mother might tell them that it's too late and that this specific adventure should be put over to another time. Or it might even be as simple as Dad suggesting he'll take his daughter out for breakfast on the way to school. Mum has already poured the milk on her daughter's bowl of cereal. 'Not today,' she might hear herself say. 'It's a bit too late.' The end result is this: the very things mothers sometimes complain about end up being the very things that we're protecting. We want a break. We want some space. We want some spontaneity injected into our lives.

And yet when it comes down to it, we too often throw cold water on the attempts men make to give us these things. 'It's not a malicious response,' one educator says. 'It's just instinctive.' And Maggie Dent says, 'We've got a fixed view of what is good and what is best, and we are not all that good at allowing men to come into that space.'

That response by the primary caregiver – usually the mother – is understandable for many reasons. She has invested so much in growing the children. She stopped having a tipple during pregnancy to give her newborn the best chance. She's sung endless songs, read innumerable storybooks, pointed out colours, and spent long nights comforting her through illness. This has been her job since withdrawing from full-time work on the birth of her daughter. She's happily sacrificed steady promotions into more challenging roles because this was best for her daughter, and she took the position of parent seriously. A dozen times a month she'd see herself reflected in her little girl and feel comfortable that her own experiences could guide her through issues as varied as being upset at what a friend said to her at lunchtime, or the fact that she was the only one in Year 6 without a smartphone. A few years down the track, when her daughter turns fifteen, she's hoping to be lucky enough for her daughter to trust her enough to reveal that she's 'a bit interested' in the boy she met at the bus stop. Of course, they'll shop for her semi-formal dress together, and plan her formal. She knows her daughter inside out, and that's taken energy, emotion, planning and a good gut feel. For someone – even her father – to walk in and up-end everything is just counterproductive.

It can be tricky for a mother to slice off a big chunk of what she sees as her responsibility – and a job at which she has worked at selflessly for years – when a father wants to take on a more substantial role. That might especially be the case if he doesn't boast the same experience. Maggie Dent says that personal investment in our daughters – and sons, for that matter – can mean we hold on too tight. This might be a hard message for women to cop. It might seem like the CEO stepping back to let a contractor take over at the office! In many cases, a father might have opted to be the provider, well aware that it meant long work hours and missing speech night. This might have suited him, too. So now, without the experience of the home's primary caregiver, he is being encouraged to come in and take on an equal role. Would he even know what to do?

As an aside, a factor that is worth mentioning here is how much mothers might live their lives through their daughters. Perhaps a mother's home finances prevented her from learning the violin in the '80s, so she is determined that her daughter has the opportunity she didn't. Or perhaps a mother had wanted to take a particular route through university, but circumstances stopped it.

Mothers in cases like these might become hell-bent on their daughter following the course that they would have liked to follow – and that can ignite fiery arguments. 'I think mothers have a greater stake in these types of things,' one long-term principal says. 'This is because she's invested more energy in making the choices – from what school her daughter goes to, to whether she does ballet or tennis or both. There's a little bit of mum trying to live out her life through her daughter,' she says. This principal reminds parents – mothers and fathers – of that at the first parent information night each year. 'I tell them that we are educating your daughter for her future, not for your past, and you need to think about that.'

Certainly society sees women as the wise heads when it comes to the management of children. But times are changing. Feminism, and what that means, is changing too. 'The old feminism was a resentment of men,' one female principal says. 'The new wave needs to be more cooperative.' Somewhere in that, men are also wanting to interpret being a father and what their masculinity means in the family context. 'I can sense something different going on where fathers are trying to get in, but women have to let them in too,' another principal says.

Ask a group of mothers, including those with full-time roles outside the home, and there is an apprehension some-times that fathers might get it wrong. They might serve up food with no nutritional value for dinner, or tell their fourteen-year-old daughter that she needs to lose weight. He might let her stay up too late on a school night, or not sign the parent consent form due on Friday. Now, accepting this is a gross generalisation, all of those things might play out to be true, and resentments can arise in the female camp. As one mother says, 'It's a bit rich claiming 50 per cent parenting at fifteen if you never got out of bed for a crying toddler!' This thinking was also borne out last year in research which showed that while men become more 'enthusiastic towards being involved in the care and upbringing of their children after experiencing parenthood, Australian women become less likely to agree that fathers should do so'. The authors say that their finding showed, in part, why partners engage in 'more traditional gender divisions of labour after parenthood'. That means a father's involvement is hampered not only by workplace or institutional factors but also 'by their female partners becoming more reluctant to support an active fathering role'.[15]

But if girls can benefit from a greater role played by their father – and that's the claim made by everyone – it has to start somewhere. Brisbane principal Toni Riordan says she's seen the frustration of fathers – particularly those of non-sporty girls – who cannot 'find a way in'. 'They know how to stand on the edge of a field and support. They don't necessarily know how to sit as an audience member in a debate or a concert,' she says.

Another principal says a study of the sideline at a weekly netball game paints a poignant picture. Fathers will take their chair and sit some distance away, often reading the paper. She says it's not because they are uninterested; they just don't know where they fit. This same principal says schools need to consider this too. 'Sometimes we might spend so much time empowering the females in our organisation – students, mothers, teachers – that we've forgotten to find the place for men,' she says. In some schools, fathers are taking matters into their own hands. In one, Maggie Dent tells me, fathers flock to the playground at lunchtime once a week. There they shoot hoops with the girls, play chess in the library and even take over the canteen. 'It just brought joy and laughter,' she says. Author and psychologist Andrew Fuller says fathers have to make the first move here. 'There's part of me that wants to say that mums aren't very good at stepping back,' he says. 'I think if the guys wait for the women to step back, they'll be waiting a long time.' That means fathers need to carve out times with their daughters consciously, but have found that difficult because there is presently no role-modelling around it. 'It doesn't occur to them to go to their daughter and say, "How about you and I go to the footy together" or "Let's go out for a bite to eat" without involving the mother as well.' Perhaps, if they did that, more mothers would see the virtue in stepping back and allowing their daughters' father to share the parenting responsibility.

Clinical psychologist Kirrilie Smout says mothers need to allow fathers increased involvement right from infancy, and need to recognise that both parents bring different assets. 'Dads have their own strengths that Mum won't have, so if you allow dads to be involved then they will be enriching your child in a way that you won't be able to do as well,' she says. She suggests couples begin by picking one area for which a father has total responsibility. Let's take teeth. He would take his daughter to the dentist, talk to the orthodontist, schedule the appointments, pay the bills and do everything else associated with it. Or perhaps he becomes Netball Dad. Leading cancer researcher and fathering expert Professor Bruce Robinson says mothers are typically gatekeepers and it is understandable that they don't want to 'lose their place'. 'Dads need to respect the valuable job they've done and not try and walk in and take over,' he says. But Professor Robinson says it is important that mothers understand the importance of a good father-figure in their daughter's life. 'We say, "Look they're your kids and you want the best for them. You're not handing over the role, you're just inviting them to take on the father-figure role that kids need.'

Sydney school leader Phillip Heath says it is important for environments to be made 'safe for dads', also. 'It's got to be okay for dads to hang out with their girls in pursuit of their experiences; that it's not just dance mums, it's everybody involved,' he says. He says success would mean that netball matches were attended by just as many male adults as female adults. In recent years, he says he's tried to change things inside his own school boundaries. 'Last year I urged the girls' football team to play on the main oval as a full-on winter experience,' he says. Goal posts were set up in front of the rugby posts and the game was played. 'As it happened, that day it was the only win we had on the main oval.' He says he later heard that, after the games, the mothers of boys and mothers of girls went out for coffee. 'The conversation around the mothers of *boys* was to lament the fact that girls had played on the main oval that day and robbed the boys of that special role they had in the school, whereas the mothers of the daughters were going, "How good was that?", "About time too".' He reiterates his point many times over. 'No mother can separate herself from her own loyalty to her child. And I think we need to recognise that – and that's why I use that word "safe" for dad.'

The word 'safe' comes up again when talking to schools about how freely they allow fathers onto school grounds. Protection policies in girls' schools are far more complicated than those in boys' schools, and the fear of an abuse allegation (and the headlines it might bring) are forefront in the minds of those who run schools. 'It's really a hard one,' one principal says. 'There is such an agenda around student protection. I'm hoping we're riding the crest of the wave at the moment and that we come down the other side and say, "Actually, this is crazy".' Another issue raised in discussions about men playing a greater role at school is the exclusive father–daughter events that are held. They are growing in number and are in demand, but still there are few compared to the number of functions, focused on mothers. 'It's so interesting how quickly women come back and say, "well what's for us?" when we're addressing what we perceive to be a disadvantage,' one school leader says.

Author and academic Dr Stephen Holden says men face barriers at home, in the same way women face them in the corporate world. We've spent so much time encouraging women into the workforce, but have we spent equivalent time supporting men to raise children? 'That's part of the piece here,' Riordan says. Fathers can work harder in this regard, too. As shown earlier, it is often fathers who decide to take that first step back from their daughters. They make the decision to abdicate to their partners, who they believe have both the confidence and the experience to deal with the parenting challenges that present themselves. 'We are poorer for it,' Dr Scott says. While warning against stereotypes, she says that women are often empowered by being the primary caregiver, and fathers can miss out, or resort to 'conditional types of transactions'. She remembers one dad who lobbed into her office. 'I'm divorcing my wife and my kids won't speak to me, so can you let them know I'm no longer going to pay the fees,' he told her. Dr Scott relates that she replied, 'Time out. What are you actually doing here? How is this going to help?'

She urges every father not to take that crucial first step back; to not retreat when parenting gets tough. 'What I would say to them is you need to be the parent. The kid doesn't get to call the shots on whether you're going to be the dad or not. That's not an autocratic, table-thumping, chest-banging thing. It is a sense that you and Mum know this kid better than anyone else on the planet. So if you step aside and let one person try to do everything, and they want that as well, you're doing an extraordinary disservice to this little person who actually wants both.' No conflict exists, she says, in loving both parents similarly. 'I deal a lot with fathers who are grief-ridden in how they are treated at times, and I just keep saying you must keep loving and loving and loving. Do not abdicate. Do not step aside. If your kid is just listening to Mum at the moment, you just keep doing the right thing. Don't sink to the level of being a child and reacting like "she hurt me so I'm going to hurt her back".' Dr Scott's passion for the role fathers should be playing in their daughters' lives is fierce. 'Don't ever let them get to the stage where they say they are not kissing you goodnight anymore. You say, "No, I'm your father and in this family we kiss goodnight" – or whatever your rules are.'

Just while we are on rules, they *are* really important, and fathers should not be afraid to impose them. Kirrilie Smout ranks 'taking charge' up there alongside fathers needing to 'connect' and 'coach' their teen girls. Rules and setting boundaries are vital. 'We want dads to say, "We have rules here about putting phones away at night, we have rules here about everyone helping in the house, we have rules here about how we talk to our family members,"' she says.

Mothers need to play ball here. They need to step back, sometimes, to let their partners step forward. That's how daughters – and indeed sons – will learn that parenting is a joint gig. 'If families get into this pattern of mothers being the one who provides the advice and are the confidantes and the father does practical things – like pays the bills and drops them to parties – I think it's then a bit difficult to expect girls to understand anything different,' one principal says. 'They expect what their parents are – the responsibility sits more with the parents than the girls.'

So how does a mother help embrace a father's willingness to parent without relinquishing her job? Beth Oakley says it's about working as a team, allowing fathers to take their daughters away camping, for example, and encouraging him to be active with them. It's not easy, she says, especially in separated families, because it might require mothers to surrender control and provide her ex-partner with ample time with his daughters. Andrew

Fuller issues a warning here, too. He says sometimes when a father re-partners, his new partner becomes the gateway between him and his biological children. That's not ideal, he says. 'In a way it's about saying, "This relationship is really important and you need to be charged with creating it."' Fathers should not worry if they don't know the latest fad, or which celebrity is doing what. 'It's about doing stuff together,' Andrew Fuller says. Maggie Dent says fathers can also feel as though they are being constantly criticised by mothers and will never measure up to the job, no matter what they do. Mothers play an important role here. 'It's about having those quiet chats . . . an honest conversation over how you can both do things better,' she says. 'If you want your daughter to be raised to be the best expression of herself, a warm relationship with her father is critical. You've got to allow that warm relationship to happen.'

Corporate Australia needs to do more here, too, not only in navigating ways for women to keep their careers but for men to have more flexibility in caregiving. Schools are doing their part, with the biggest chunk of wellbeing budgets going towards parent education. Parents are hungry for it, partly because of the massive changes brought on by technology, and those issues that target this generation more than the last: body image, online safety, anxiety . . . the list goes on. It makes sense, then, that parenting also needs to fit the times. Brisbane principal

Catherine O'Kane uses that term 'agile parenting' – a take on the current focus on 'agile leadership'. Think of the time and money schools plough into the professional development of their staff to ensure they are up to date with best practice. The same goes with training in the public service, and investment in private business. Leadership requires agility and flexibility, and the influence of new technology has driven the need for good leaders to know how to change direction smartly. Why would parenting be any different? 'A lot of people go into it thinking it's one thing – this is the way I parent and I have to be consistent across all my children – and I agree with that as well, but we have to change as the challenges change for our children,' O'Kane says. Kirrilie Smout says we've all heard parents say, 'My parents didn't even know what year I was in and I turned out okay', but all relationships need work. You work at being a better partner or being a better employer. 'And you can get better at being a better parent too,' she says. 'It's a skill level I think we can all improve on.'

How we approach our daughters between the ages of ten and seventeen is profoundly unique, and it does require genuine agility. At ten, girls are wanting their parents' guidance as they navigate friendships and learn decision-making skills. Rules are so important here, too, but so is how flexible parents are as increased independence is granted during the teen years. By seventeen, girls are capable of making important life decisions for themselves. One example given frequently is of parents, well-meaning, choosing the career path for their daughters – despite the school guidance officers hearing their daughters wanting something very different. 'I can tell you from my own anecdotal knowledge it never works,' O'Kane says, when asked. By seventeen, girls are young women with a free will, and hopefully the analytical skills born of a good education. Parents can influence and cajole and hope, but they also have to be willing to accept when the decision is not the one they might have chosen.

Practice makes perfect, Dr Scott says. And perhaps that's the message for men and women, raising children. 'If you don't have practice then you're not going to get better. You're going to keep using the same tools you've always had in the hope that if you just speak a little louder or you thump the table a little more, the message will get through.' She says all parents need to be allowed to fail, and for that not to become an enormous deal. 'I've made so many mistakes with my kids but because I have been with them constantly I can moderate my behaviour. I learn when not to push, when to push. I'm constantly practising – whereas I don't think the men sometimes are given that opportunity,' she says.

16

Thank you, Dad

The girls in this group are fidgeting. It's the first time they've stopped talking in forty-five minutes. A piece of paper and a pen sits in front of each of them, and, so far, it's blank. On this occasion it's a group of fourteen- to sixteen-year-olds at an all-girls school in Queensland, but it could be any group, at any school, in any state. The response is silence. To other questions, the girls haven't stopped talking, giving examples and comparing their fathers to the peer sitting alongside them. What do you admire about your father? How could he try more? What could you do better? When last did you talk to your dad without interruption for ten minutes? What's his best dad joke? Do you think he parents you the same as your brothers? Who do you go to first, with a problem? The answers storm out. 'My father's more over-protective than yours!' 'I hardly ever see Dad. He's always at work!' 'I can tell my dad anything.' 'I haven't seen mine in three years. I miss him.'

But this question has stumped them: *What would you like to tell your father if you knew he was listening to you?* To be honest, I thought I knew exactly what their answer would be. A year before, I had asked other groups of fourteen-year-old girls similar questions. When they were asked how they thought they would parent their own teen daughter down the track, three answers stood out: they vowed to listen more, to spend more time with them, and to let them make mistakes. With another group, I asked them to jot down what they would like to tell their parents. Almost unanimously, those girls wrote the note to their mother, not their father. And the overwhelming answer was this: *Listen to me. Listen to what I am saying. Hear what I am telling you. Listen but don't judge.* They hadn't taken more than a moment to answer the question. So why, when asked the same question about their fathers, was this group of girls so reluctant to respond?

The answer is that, for most of them, any personal response breached the norm of what they'd usually talk about with their dad. It wasn't sport, or current affairs, or homework. How would they go about telling their father something much more personal? And how would that conversation begin? To almost every girl in the room, it was not a conversation that they believed was needed or that they would countenance. It would be much easier, they said, to talk about this stuff with their mother. Conversations with Dad were more transactional.

With encouragement, answers start trickling in. 'My dad smokes and I'd ask him to stop smoking,' one younger girl says. So why not ask him? 'Because maybe he won't stop,' she says. Another says her father would be surprised if she turned up and announced she loved him – which is what she would say if she could. 'He'd wonder why I randomly said it.'

The literal answers of the younger girls are delightful. 'Why aren't I as tanned as you?' 'Can I have a trampoline, and oh, don't die.' 'Let me get wi-fi and Netflix pleeease.' 'Can I have a dog?' All of these relate to something concrete. But the answers from those a bit older are more poignant and surprising in equal measure. The number-one thing girls would say to their fathers, if they could, is 'thank you'. Number two is an expression of love, and number three is a plea to spend more time with them, followed by a strong request by girls who had absent fathers or lived in separated families that their voice be heard.

It's worth hearing girls say it in their own words.

'Thank you for everything you do for me and sorry if I don't say that enough.'

'I'd like to say, Dad, thank you for everything you've done. I may not show that I appreciate it but I do. I look up to you and I find it really hard sometimes when you go away, even though you've been doing it all my life.'

'You provide us with more than anyone could possibly dream of. THANK YOU.'

'That I'm thankful for everything he does.'

'Thank him for everything.'

'Thanks for being there for me.'

'Thank you for everything, you have no idea how much I appreciate everything you do and say to me and I'm scared I'll never be able to thank you properly for all that.'

'I would love to tell him how much he means to me and that I am grateful for every sacrifice he has made for me and his family.'

'I would like to say thank you for always being there for me and I wish that you take some time out to spend with Mum and I.'

'Thanks for being a cool dad.'

'I'd just say thanks for everything; driving me everywhere. It's such a regular thing that you don't think twice about it.'

Given the plea I'd heard girls make a year earlier for their mums to listen to what they wanted to tell them, without judgement, it flummoxed me that girls were so keen – remember this was the most common answer – to thank Dad. My bewilderment was shared by others. 'Perhaps they don't spend much time with their fathers so they are more appreciative of any time he gives,' one teen expert opined. Other suggestions popped up too. 'I wonder if sometimes the dads do less of the disciplining,' one deputy principal said. 'I've heard various stories that Dad often builds that relationship by being the one who spoils and gives in a little bit more than Mum does.' This principal's response was a question, not an answer: 'Do they see Dad as the breadwinner working so hard to support the family? They're saying thanks for life and material goods, rather than the relationship?' Another expert said, 'It's taken for granted that women will do most things. Mum is the one who will drop something in to school if you forget it. A lot of dads tend to get the pleasant extras.' And a member of the wellbeing staff at one school commented, 'I can only guess that it's "I know you've got so much else to do so when you give up time and make it about me, I'm so grateful for that."'

Toowoomba principal Dr Linda Evans says: 'Girls crave doing things with their fathers and that's what they love. There's less conversation and there's more doing. Irrespective of the liberation of women, it's still mothers who do more of the domestic stuff.' She remembers picking up her own daughter when she was in high school and being told that she had a dozen or more parties to attend on the weekend. 'And I'd be saying "no" and we'd argue all the way home. We'd fall into that pattern. She wouldn't do that with her father, but she'd do it with me.' Another principal says you could sometimes see that teen girls believe that 'when Dad turns up to something, it's more special than if Mum turns up'. She also says, 'I reckon it's "whenever I'm with Mum I'm being organised. I'm expected to do this and I'm expected to do that. If I go with Dad it's just going to be fun, because he doesn't worry about all that stuff."' That rings true, according to those mothers with whom I discussed this response. One makes the point that a weekend away usually sees Mum do the packing. That night, around the campfire, Dad will toast marshmallows for everyone – "as long as someone's remembered to pack them",' she quips. 'His tasks are more responsive and mums are more organisational.'

Dad is often more fun, too. Melbourne principal Polly Flanagan remembers overhearing a conversation between her then-twelve-year-old daughter and her friend in the back of the car many years ago. 'They were talking about who they would go with, if their parents divorced, and my daughter said, "I'd go with Dad. He's more entertaining." I nearly ran off the road. Here is Mum's taxi service. I was probably going to the supermarket and then I was probably going to pay some bills and then to pick them up from wherever they were going . . .' Most mothers reading those comments will nod in agreement. Daughters can be their mother's harshest critics, a point Melbourne principal Marise McConaghy has noticed over many years teaching in different schools. 'They've all forgiven their mothers now – but my goodness, in Years 10 and 11 and 12, if their mothers worked they were hopeless and if they didn't work they were even more hopeless.' But that changes, she says, as they grow and see life through a more mature prism. It is still difficult for women, though, particularly those trying to balance full-time work with the primary-caregiver role at home. If you have three children to wrangle and an important work project due, 'fun' might not make the priority list.

Put to them, the girls agree. 'I think I do judge Mum more. Dad is kind of cool. Mum, I don't know, she's just not cool,' Stacey says. Her friend joins in: 'I'm the same. Mum always jumps in and puts her two cents in, which is always annoying. I'm with her a lot more than my dad because she drives me to school and back.' There's a theme developing around the table now. 'My whole family is a tennis family,' Andrea says. 'But I feel when my mother is commenting on how I play and what I can do to improve, I take it more personally – as though she's insulting what

I'm doing. Whereas if my dad was to do it, I'd be more likely to take it on board.' Why? 'I don't know. He is the better player in the family.' Holly: 'I don't know if I judge her more, but she's more embarrassing. Like if my friends come over, she's talking to them, but Dad just stays in his room.' Adele: 'I disagree more with my mum. I'm more like my dad.' And so it goes . . . Emma explains how her mother will jump to criticism, first, where her father would be more 'chilled'. She gives the example of playing basketball. 'Mum will say, "Why did you do that?" or "You should have done that". Dad would just make a side comment and leave it at that.'

Gold Coast principal Dr Julie Wilson Reynolds says she feels it's a shame that girls will so quickly dismiss the contribution made by their mothers. 'Mums need a lot of thanks,' she says. Vivienne Durham, from the Girls' Schools Association, UK, says girls' views of their mothers are often matched by boys' views of their fathers. 'What you see is your role model,' she says. 'The parent of your own gender is your direct role model very often, and you're a harsh critic of it – you're competing with it, it's what you are growing away from.' She says often fathers also become 'putty in their daughters' hands'. She tells of fathers who run companies worth hundreds of millions of dollars and employ thousands of employees. 'The girls could essentially run rings around them,' she says. New Zealand educator Tom Matthews says: 'If I ignore my children and then give them praise, that's going to feel really significant. Whereas if I'm constantly giving that same gift every day, then I will become a bit complacent and critical and feel safer in the relationship to be critical.'

So, with 'Thank you, Dad' the number-one message girls want to deliver to their fathers, 'I love you' comes in a strong second. Here's a sample of the responses to the question, *What would you like to tell your father if you could?*

'That I love him. I never say it because it's too hard. And that I wish he would be here forever until I die, and I'm going to be really upset when he's gone, so let's make the most of the time we have together and never be upset or angry with each other.'

'He should know that I love him infinitely and that I am grateful for all the opportunities he provides for me, even if I may not show it.'

'I would like to say I appreciate everything he does and that I love him more than he can imagine.'

'That I really love him, even when I get angry.'

'Will you always love me?'

'I love you and I wish I could say it more often. It's just a bit awks.'

'That I love him more than life itself, but sometimes I just need to be a girl. I need to cry. I need to feel depressed in order to be happy. He may have gone through the same thing almost forty years ago, but the times are different and he needs to see that. But I will always love him with all my heart. No matter what.'

'Shut the f__ up and just listen to what I have to say for a moment before you blow your top. Also, I love you.'

Spending more time together is certainly a priority, too. No doubt exists that girls feel that the lack of time they spend with their fathers directly impacts on the relationship they share. It creates a gap. It leads, in some cases, to a superficial bond where conversations are rarely personal. It means girls can also find their father unapproachable. So many of them want that to change.

'I would just like to tell him that I would love to spend more time with him . . . I am not sure if he knows that.'

'I would ask him to be less angry when I have swimming or netball on, and to ask me if I'm okay when I'm feeling upset, and spend more time with me instead of doing work on the computer. But I would never have the guts to tell him that.'

'Hey, maybe find a job that you enjoy so you don't have to be out as much and I can spend more time with you.'

'If he could spend less time on his job and spend more time with my brother and me?'

'Can you please spend more time with me?'

'Dad, why is it that you're always busy playing chess downstairs in your man cave when all I want to do is spend time with you?'

'Dad, I'm only going to be young once and I really want to spend as much time with you as I can, but you need to lighten up and not always think about saving money for the future, but rather enjoying the present.'

The plea for time is deafening, yet on a daily basis at home, a girl is unlikely to make that obvious. She might spend her spare time in her room, with the door closed. Or on her phone, chatting to friends. Or at a friend's home. But given the option, these girls are asking – and in such a mature way – their fathers to be around more often.

The fourth most common answer is worth recording, because it follows on from the 'want more time' answer. These responses come from girls who do not live with their father, or feel as though they never see him. It takes a hard heart not to be moved by these answers.

'I hate the fact that you're not around and the fact that you never call on the days you say, but mostly I hate the fact that I don't hate you, not even a little bit.'

'I want to live with you.'

'I miss you and wish you could work in Melbourne.'

'Stop worrying and please move to Adelaide.'

'That it hurts not to remember a happy family.'

'I really wish you would've shown up when it mattered.'

'That I miss him a lot and wish he was nearby, and that I love him.'

'Please pay Child Support.'

'I would prefer you to be in my life or not at all. Choose. Either you pick up the slack or abandon me altogether. I don't need you; you are not a necessity in my life, you are simply a variable that acts as if they were more. If you really want me to be your daughter, then act like it.'

'That I hate how him and Mum fight and that I know how he is feeling but I feel like he doesn't understand how my sister and I feel and that I love him very much but it's hard and that he means the world to me and I cannot explain how much I appreciate him for always being there for us.'

'Don't just put money in my bank account to think I will forgive you. Get to know me.'

'Do you miss spending time with me or wish I would be with you more?'

'I wish you and Mum didn't break up.'

Of course, talking to so many girls – 1200 by survey and more than 100 in person – is going to raise more answers than it is possible to publish. But these were typical. Many of the other themes that cropped up have been addressed in earlier chapters. They all show the importance of fathers and daughters staying connected and refusing to allow the onset of adolescence to create a divide. Perhaps in that way it's like any adult relationship: it needs to be fed and nurtured. Hard words are stewed on, silence creates distance. If I've learnt anything from this task it's that girls don't want that distance to develop, and if it does then they find it hard to go back. They want to connect, and reconnect. They find that difficult and awkward, but they are children. Surely the responsibility for the first move rests with their parents, or in the case at hand, their fathers?

So what else might your daughter be wanting you to talk about? Here are some of the other answers (and questions) provided by the girls.

'That I am not straight.'

'Why do you always pick my brother over me?'

'You made me the person I am today.'

'You need to trust that I am doing the right thing. I am trying so hard, and yes, I procrastinate and I can be a failure, but I'm trying . . . But we're fine. I still love you.'

'Everyone is valid. Muslims are allowed to wear burkas, gay people are allowed to get married, women do not need to be protected by men any more than men need to be protected by women.'

'That he needs to listen and be more caring of me, and that I do thank him and do love him.'

'What do you think of me, not just as your daughter but as a person?'

'Even though I already tell my dad almost anything, I guess the thing I wish I could ask him would be if I make him proud. I try my best with everything I do but sometimes I feel as though I am never doing enough to please my dad and to make him proud of me, which gets me down a lot but I never show it because I want him to always see me happy.'

'I don't want to take over the family company.'

'I would like to say that although I respect your opinions I think that you need to be more open in your opinions, as you are alway telling me to be.'

'Please don't expect me to be perfect. I will always make mistakes but I fix them and learn from them.'

'Ask me questions. Show you're interested.'

'I would like to say that I am getting older and he needs to let me go from being the five-year-old I used to be.'

'Sometimes you just need to be a little less protective. I know you love me but I need to make mistakes to learn.'

'To try and focus on having a fluent and easy conversation or communication, whether that's just talking about what we are eating at dinner or expanding off a comment I will say. I would also tell him to keep trying to get through to me. I know I can be a moody bitch and I know I am short-tempered with him, but it's hard for me to control my emotions and I still need him in my life.'

'Man up and start making a proper effort. I will acknowledge and feel more loved if you put in more effort. Stop asking me what I want you to do. Think about what I love. For example, come and support me at my hockey match without me specifically asking you to.'

'I'm sorry for all the times I've been hard on him. After I've had a bad day and he comes home from work, I take it out on him. I feel guilty the next day but don't know how to say sorry.'

'That I'm proud of him – for how hard he works and how he raised my brother and me. I haven't said that because you need the right place.'

The right place, according to every expert, for father and daughter, is here and now.

17

Never too late

It can't ever be easy telling someone they're dying, but Dr Bruce Robinson, a professor of medicine, has done it more times than he cares to remember. 'The process of breaking bad news is probably the most intimate moment a doctor has with anybody,' he says. 'It's so important to do well.' So important, in fact, that for the past twenty-five years this former WA Australian of the Year has run medical-school courses on how to do it.

When it comes to breaking the news to fathers, Dr Robinson says the conversation unfolds much the same way each time, and that's with a father sitting opposite him declaring that if he could steal back time, he'd spend it with his children. 'To be honest, it breaks my heart,' he says. He remembers one patient wondering why he always thought work was his chief priority. 'Why didn't someone put their hands on my shoulders and say, "Mate, it's important, but it's not that important," he asked his surgeon.

Asked what fathers in 2018 don't get when it comes to raising daughters and Bruce Robinson articulates the same answer as experts around the country. 'First of all, they don't realise how important they are. They think somehow they're the icing on the cake and Mum's the sort of lynchpin of it all. They do not realise how profoundly important they are – how she feels about her looks, what they can do for her confidence and particularly how she is going to engage with men,' he says. 'And secondly, they don't know what to do. They've lived a boy's life, not a girl's – and that's only magnified if they've attended an all-boys school, or not had sisters.'

During this project, not too many fathers told me they saw themselves as crucial to their daughters' lives. Many of them had felt they were crucial once upon a time, but now, with their daughters travelling through the tween years and into adulthood, they somehow felt less important. Just as rare were dads who believed they had the fathering gig in the bag. Indeed, the list of questions raised by fathers ran to pages and pages. 'How do I handle it if she doesn't get the results she wants at the end of Year 12?' 'How do I speak to her regarding relationships with boys?' 'How do I be more positive without condoning poor behaviour?' 'How does she get the confidence to believe in herself?' 'How do I get her off social media?' 'How do I talk to her about managing stress and female-to-female relationships?' 'How do I help her with her body negativity.' 'Where do I start?'

I've tried to start at the beginning because I've learnt through this year-long research project that it is never too late for a father or father-figure to build on the relationship he has with his daughter. That's because this connection follows girls into their twenties, thirties, forties and fifties. Indeed, it colours their whole life, influencing how they behave, how they see men (including partners) and, if unresolved, how they parent their own children.

It's not only the experts – principals, psychologists, parenting professionals, doctors and academics – who say that. It stands out in the pleas of so many of the 1300 girls involved in this book. They want their father and they need him – even if it doesn't look like that. But the potential for a magic father–daughter relationship also shines strongly in the petition of almost 400 fathers whose views are also aired here.

So here's a tip sheet of ten skills to help fathers rekindle (or never lose) that charming bond that shines out in early family photographs.

1. Love her unconditionally – and make sure she knows that. Tell her. Make sure she knows that love is

stronger than any other emotion that might pull you away from her.

2. A father has the power to build a girl's confidence, or crush it. Value her opinion. Encourage her to speak out with respectful and considered views, even if they don't match your own.

3. Whether you live under the same roof or not, you have a responsibility to be there. *Really* be there. Do not – despite any encouragement from your daughter – take a step back.

4. Pick an interest or a project and develop it with her. A love of Ed Sheeran's music, or a weekly park run, a charity project – build memories together.

5. Don't fix her problems; listen to her, and teach her the skills to evaluate and make good decisions. While you are doing that, teach her to change a car tyre and replace a light bulb!

6. A daughter is not weaker or more vulnerable than her brother. She is different, but not inferior in any way. Be ambitious for her.

7. A father is a girl's prime role model for men. This gives fathers an extraordinary power. She will learn what to expect from men from you and how you treat her, her mother and other women.

8. Take your daughter on dates, by herself, and tell her she's special. Make sure she knows that the two of you have a bond separate from anyone else.

9. Fathers offer their daughters lessons and skills their mothers cannot provide. (Of course, the opposite is true too.) You can be a provider and a parent!

10. Talk. Communicate. Say things. Have conversations. Chat. Remember that males and females communicate in very different ways, so it's important to understand that and find a way through it.

Providing an unshakeable foundation for a robust, warm and lifelong bond between father and daughter might actually take a lifetime to get right, but you'll see proof of your hard work in the awesome woman who calls you Dad.

Endnotes

1. Elizabeth L Barrett and Mark T Morman, 'Turning Points of Closeness in the Father/Daughter Relationship', *Human Communication*, Vol. 15, No. 4, pp. 241–259.
2. Newshub, 'Young girls feel pressured to be perfect on social media: Girl Guides New Zealand', 12 May 2017 <http://www.newshub.co.nz/home/entertainment/2017/05/young-girls-feel-pressured-to-be-perfect-on-social-media-girl-guides-new-zealand.html>.
3. Linda Nielsen, 'How Dads Affect Their Daughters into Adulthood', Institute for Family Studies, 3 June 2014.
4. Jackie Bischof, 'Here's what dads can do at home to help their daughters grow into successful leaders', Quartz, 28 August 2016 <https://qz.com/768456/heres-what-dads-can-do-at-home-to-help-their-daughters-grow-into-successful-leaders/>.
5. Henrik Cronqvist and Frank Yu, 'Company chiefs with daughters make for kinder workplaces', The Conversation, 15 July 2015 <https://theconversation.com/company-chiefs-with-daughters-make-for-kinder-workplaces-44512>.
6. Jennifer Baxter, Lyndall Strazdins and Jianghong Li, 'Long Hours and Longing', Australian Institute of Family Studies, September 2017.

7. 'Marriages and Divorces, Australia, 2016', Australian Bureau of Statistics <http://www.abs.gov.au/ausstats/abs@.nsf/mf/3310.0>.
8. Linda Nielsen, 'How daughters can repair a damaged relationship with their divorced dad', The Conversation, 11 July 2017 <https://theconversation.com/how-daughters-can-repair-a-damaged-relationship-with-their-divorced-dad-80634>.
9. Mirjana Majdandžić et al, 'The Structure of Challenging Parenting Behavior and Associations With Anxiety in Dutch and Australian Children', *Journal of Clinical Child & Adolescent Psychology*, 20 October 2017 <https://www.mq.edu.au/newsroom/2017/12/12/encouraging-risk-taking-in-children-may-reduce-the-prevalence-of-childhood-anxiety/>.
10. 'Teachers and fathers play key roles in preventing cyberbullying', University of Hertfordshire, 22 June 2017 <http://www.herts.ac.uk/about-us/news/2017/june/teachers-and-fathers-play-key-roles-in-protecting-young-people-from-cyberbullying>.
11. Jennifer Kromberg 'How Dads Shape Daughters' Relationships', *Psychology Today*, 1 July 2013 <https://www.psychologytoday.com/blog/inside-out/201307/how-dads-shape-daughters-relationships>.
12. Linda Nielsen, 'How Dads Affect Their Daughters into Adulthood', Institute for Family Studies, 3 June 2014.
13. Jennifer Baxter et al, 'Long Hours and Longing', Australian Institute of Family Studies, 2017.
14. Australian Institute of Family Studies, 'Stay-at-home Dads', May 2017 <http://aifs.gov.au/publications/stay-home-dads>.
15. Sandra Buchler et al, 'Does Parenthood Change Attitudes to Fathering? Evidence from Australia and Britain', *Sex Roles* <https://link.springer.com/article/10.1007/s11199-017-0757-8>.

Acknowledgements

This book could only happen because of the girls and fathers who believed in it; almost 1700 of them answered my long list of questions. Their identities are all protected here, but their honesty was as revealing, as was it humbling. Fathers who pleaded for an answer to find a way back into their daughters' lives. Fathers who were questioning the views of the strong independent daughter they'd raised. Fathers who enjoyed a good bond, but wanted to insure it against breaking. Fathers who were separated and who were lost, as their daughters travelled from toddler to teenager. Daughters, too, wanted to understand their father better: why he was more over-protective of her than her brother; why he was always busy; why their relationship might not hold the magic it had a decade earlier. Thank you for asking the questions and I hope the answers provided by the experts in this book do justice to them.

We are lucky so many experts practise in this area and *Fathers and Daughters* is better for the generosity of their time, experience and ideas. People like Professor Bruce Robinson, a leading cancer researcher, medico and a former WA Australian of the Year, who founded the Fathering Project to encourage fathers and father-figures to become better dads. I met so many outstanding individuals dedicating their work lives to the growth of our children and they deserve more recognition than they get. The time I spent with Maggie Dent, Andrew Fuller, Paul Dillon, Kirrilie Smout and Dr Justin Coulson informs this book. So do the views of Mark McCrindle, Dr Steve Hambleton, Dr Katherine Main, Associate Professor Michael Nagel, Dr Stephen Holden, John Gray, Professor Gayle Kaufman, Professor Ruben Gur, Dr Vaughan Cruickshank, Dr Jennifer Mascaro and Dr Terry Fitzsimmons. Bodies like the Alliance of Girls' Schools Australasia, and particularly Loren Bridge, whose focus is on educating and growing strong women. The Australian Institute of Family Studies, especially Jenny Baxter and Lixia Qu, offer a gold mine of research, that every parent should use, more often. Thank you.

My last book, *Being 14*, taught me how willing schools are to engage in any discussion that advances their students' lives. It was no different this time round, and my thanks go to all the principals, school leaders and welfare officers who sat through long interviews, and 'tolerated' the calls that followed to check issues. Former principals with decades of experience, like Robyn Kronenberg and Dr Tim Hawkes, also saw the value in this project and supported it with enormous generosity of time and effort. Kevin Tutt and Sue Chandler were among those who read this manuscript, in an earlier form, and their suggestions improved it. The words of wisdom from many educators are chronicled on these pages. Others preferred to provide their expertise anonymously. I am equally appreciative.

A book is produced by a team, not an author, and my thanks go to the wonderful team at Hachette Australia: Vanessa Radnidge, my publisher, whose optimism is contagious; Lydia Tasker, who treats every book she publicises as her very own; Tom Bailey-Smith who never tires – at least it seems that way – of authors' questions; Susan Gray, whose edits have made this book much more readable. To Justin Ractliffe, Louise Sherwin-Stark, Fiona Hazard, Christa Moffitt, Isabel Staas, Daniel Pilkington, Louise McClean and the rest of the team at Hachette, it's a partnership I truly value.

Finally, to my family: David Fagan, my partner in life, love and parenting, and our two gorgeous teen girls, Maddie and Siena, who make our world go round. Read this: it will be worth it.

Index

'not sweat the small stuff'
118–19

Oakley, Beth 66, 221–3, 238,
252
Oaten, Jennifer 149, 151, 195
O'Kane, Catherine 12, 51–2,
198, 254–5
one-parent family 157–8
openness 56, 203
opposing views 192–9
over-protective *see* protectiveness

parent-anxiety 76
parent network 29–30
parenting by gender 174–9,
185–90
parenting issues 5, 12, 51–2
partner influence 4
peer group pressure 8
perception 79–80
'permanence', understanding of
25
personality differences 51
phone 2
physical contact 48
  male teachers 130–3
poor judgment 8
pornography 209, 210–12
practical help 71
problem solving 200–1, 275
protectiveness 172–90, 275
protectors 35
provider or parent 224–40, 276
puberty 20–3
punishment 53

raunch culture 207–12
re-engagement 33, 39
rejection, fear of 74
relational pattern characteristics
213
respect 197–8, 218
Riordan, Toni 48, 63, 246, 250
risk-taking 23–4
Rite Journey 113–14
Robinson, Professor Bruce 248,
272–3
role modelling 82, 124–8,
218–20, 230, 275
Rouse, Detective Inspector Jon
207, 210–12, 237
Royal Commission into sexual
abuse of children 131
rules 252

'safe risk-taking' 187–8
safety 8
saying no 201
school
  events 109, 250
  male teachers 129–33
  parent education 253–4
  parent-friendly 237–8
  parental engagement 125–6,
  230–5
  protection policies 13, 235,
  248–50
  role of 12
Scott, Dr Briony 52–3, 54, 77,
115, 166–7, 201, 241–2,
250–1, 255

Resources

If you or your daughter are in difficulty, or just need someone to talk to, there are people who can help.

Kids Helpline Australia
kidshelpline.com.au or 1800 55 1800

Kidsline New Zealand
kidsline.org.nz or 0800 54 37 54

MensLine Australia
mensline.org.au or 1300 78 99 78

Father & Child Trust New Zealand
fatherandchild.org.nz

Lifeline Australia
lifeline.org.au or 13 11 14

Lifeline Aotearoa
lifeline.org.nz or 0800 543 354

beyondblue

beyondblue.org.au or 1300 22 4636

National Depression Initiative New Zealand

depression.org.nz or 0800 111 757

BEING 14

Helping fierce teens become awesome women

> 'A deeply thoughtful and enlightening exploration of the world of 14-year-old girls.'
>
> Marise McConaghy –
> Principal, Strathcona Girls'
> Grammar in Victoria

Is your daughter 14?
Are you struggling to know what's going on inside her head?
Are you worried?

Being 14 can help you understand how she's feeling, what she's thinking and what you need to do to help her navigate her tricky teens to become an awesome woman.

Award-winning journalist, author and commentator Madonna King has interviewed two hundred 14-year-old girls and talked to leading psychologists, school principals, CEOs, police, guidance counsellors and neuroscientists to reveal the social, psychological and physical challenges every 14-year-old girl is facing today. *Being 14* gives a voice to those teen girls and tells you:

- How much independence does she need?
- The power of her friendship group
- How you can help build her self-confidence
- Why the obsession with selfies, social media and FOMO?
- How parents unknowingly make life so much harder for her

This is what every 14-year-old girl wants her mum or dad to know, and what every parent needs to read.

'valuable for any parents of teens or pre-teens'
Sunday Times

'. . . a comprehensive guide for parents in understanding what daughters need to grow into awesome women'
New Idea

'If you have a young teenage daughter, this book will help you navigate those complex, challenging years.'
Good Health

Shortlisted for the 2018 ABIA Award for General Non-Fiction

hachette
AUSTRALIA

If you would like to find out more about Hachette Australia, our authors, upcoming events and new releases you can visit our website or our social media channels:

hachette.com.au

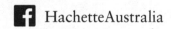 HachetteAustralia

 HachetteAus